Welcome & Thanks...

Thank you for purchasing th...
We appreciate your support...
the best guide book but continue our efforts to make Fruita one of
the best singletrack destinations in the world.

Thanks for your support and we hope you enjoy what we have
done so far. Welcome...

Guidebook Text by: Troy Rarick
Editing, Maps, and Cover Design by: Anne Keller
Cover artwork by: Sheryl Chapman

Contents

How to use this book...

Hello, I am Troy, the author of this guide book. Not to 'toot my horn' but so you'll understand some of my passion within this book: I also developed/helped develop many of the trails you'll find here. Because of that you'll find much passion about preserving them and a tremendous sense of pride in what they have become: a world cycling destination. In hopes of helping you interpret this 'local knowledge,' here are some tips on using this book.

The fact sheet is at the top of each page. Here's what it tells you...

What is it: A quick idea of what this ride is about
Where do I start: Where to park your car
How song: In miles; hours are too subjective
Climbing: How much gain in feet, how high at the top
Highlight: The part you'll talk about afterward
Who rides this: I try to describe the skill/strength needed
Why it's cool: What it is that makes this worth riding
When to ride: When these rides are good. (Note: when we have mud it is **awful**. Please don't try to ride in the mud. It ruins trails, bikes and days off.)

I use mileage, but definitely do not want this book to be a 'computer required' guidebook. I don't use one and you won't need one. I try to communicate with trail logic. If it says nothing about the intersection, then the intersection is either new or you don't turn there. If you get confused, read ahead, and it will usually make sense. Pay special attention to when I say 'turn right, climbing/descending' – that will help you know where you are and what to do.

Bottom line — most of these rides are very easy to follow and very hard to ever get lost on. The ones that require special concern say so; don't ignore that. And do take a Latitude 40 Fruita/GJ map; it may save you a cold night. **Our hand-drawn maps for this guidebook are a reference, but like all hand-drawn maps, are not quite to scale and should not be the source of blame should you happen to get yourself lost.** Your best help will be to get some local direction/advice. We don't mind. Over the Edge is staffed with riders and trail builders and is willing and equipped to help you.

RIDE ON!

Introduction

This is Fruita, Colorado, an MTB destination born out of passion for the sport. Welcome to Fruita and the fifth — –and best – edition of the Fruita Fat Tire Guide.

An original – that's Fruita, that's Over the Edge Sports, the Fruita Fat Tire Festival and this book. It's never been cool in Fruita to do it the old way nor the easy way. We didn't find trails, we built them; we didn't find a place, we made one; and we didn't let some newcomer lackey write our guide book; we wrote it ourselves. So yes, the grammar could be better and the pictures could be too. But each page is stained with the dirt of these trails and the passion of the folks who built them. Thanks for buying our book – let the lackeys starve!

The Fruita story is almost backwards. It was the recognition of the potential and the area itself that led to the establishment of a business, the Bike shop 'Over the Edge Sports,' which opened in 1995. It was then that the shop founder, Troy Rarick, with many Fruita and Grand Junction locals set out to build a new trail system and radically push the expansion of the existing areas. Once we began we recognized the need for some information and maps to get people to these trails. Pages of scribbled maps and verbal directions worked for a time but the need for written directions gave birth to this book.

I'm Troy; this is my book. Not a collection of trails I put together and not a 're-done' half plagiarized version of a guide book taken from someone else's hard work. No, this is the book that gave birth to every other Fruita book. It is written with the help of the people who have the dirt of every one of these trails still under our nails and in our hearts. I am proud of this book and I sincerely hope you find it a bit different than the norm but still a fun and useful tool to find the singletrack adventure you seek in Fruita, Colorado.

Because we actually live here, hope to make our living here, and welcome you here as well, you will find many mentions in this book about taking care of this place. Please give those 'ethics' a serious look. It is so easy to think that your impact won't hurt anything, but just remember there are 30,000 of us each year. Suddenly, each gathered piece of firewood or 'off trail track' adds up to epic decline of the very things that make Fruita cool... narrow singletrack and pure scenic high desert environment. We fight hard for it. Thanks for helping us spread the word and take care of it.

So, this is Fruita. You're probably tired of reading and ready to get out and see why so many come ride here and love it enough to tell you about it. It may be odd to mention here but I will anyway: I like having you here. It's important for you to know that, because that's why we make such a big deal out of 'low impact' ethics. We all hate the towns that hate the tourists – I know I do. But you're guests, my guests if you like. Thanks for taking good care of our fragile trails and please let me know if I or any of us can make your time here better.

Sounds cheesy? I hope not, cause here it's sincere. It's a bit different. It's original. It's Fruita. So there we go – come help us celebrate 10 years of Fruita, join us for a festival at the end of April, and... let's go ride! Oh, and by the way...

Fruita Singletrack Rules!

Fruita History

The history of mountain biking in the Grand Valley and Fruita is as hard to define as the history of the sport in general. Many have been honored and many take the credit but that is not the point. I remember having the hair brained idea in 1975 to take bikes camping on the Grand Mesa and riding west bench trail singletrack as two adventure-seeking kids just looking for some fun. Truth is, that's where our sport came from. Not from me or anyone else but from the hearts of kids and the mixed affection for bikes and dirt. Well, Fruita/Grand Junction is the same; just some great folks looking for fun on bikes in the splendid dirt of western Colorado.

The earliest credit for mountain biking in Fruita/Grand Junction probably must include Crested Butte. We all know that CB was key in the revolution that is now our sport. With them so close to us, the riders' enthusiasm rubbed off. People from the Butte came to ride or moved here and brought the passion with them. People like Barb Bowman, who came from CB, brought familiarity with mountain biking and became valuable allies in the development of the MTB scene and trail system here.

1987 brought about the beginning of this area taking a lead role in MTB development. I know that many were involved in the idealizing and completion of the Kokopelli's trail from Fruita to Moab, including 11 miles of really tough singletrack. The trail opened officially in 1989 and became a national MTB destination and the beginning of it all. COPMOBA stayed together and is still the advocacy group in our area and has been instrumental in almost all our trails and maintenance efforts in recent years.

1995 was the year Over the Edge Sports emerged on the scene. The small shop in Fruita set out on a frenzied pace of building trails, writing down information and letting the secret out about the magic in the area. It was this vision and energy that lead to the development of the Bookcliffs area, and together with COPMOBA and The Bike Patrol we have developed one of the best trail systems in the world...and we are not done yet.

In 1996 we launched the first Fruita Fat Tire Festival and as a result landed on the cover of *Bicycling Magazine* with the headline "Paradise Found" (thanks Rich & Fred). The Fest was a hit and as the word spread a destination MTB town was born.

7

All the trails in the area were built by the hands of the local MTB community. Some say the Boockliffs were just cow trails; well not really. Although that is what we found out there, and we started out riding them, the trails there now demonstrate a flow that I've never seen in a cow. The locals are and should be proud of our trails here. They put in tremendous hours of work and still do. It is important to realize that. This is not an area built for the people by some agency; these trails were built for you, by us – enjoy them and take care of them and the strong roots of Fruita.

As the author of this book I could fill it's pages with the credits and tales of the experience of "Building Fruita," something I will be proud of my whole life. From a bankrupt town to an international destination – hard to imagine. But it comes from the trails, and the trails come from the people, and therein lies the strength of Fruita, Colorado. So as you ride here I hope you appreciate where we came from. As you meet the locals I hope you appreciate them for all they have done for all of us. As you enjoy Fruita or other places like it, show your respect for the history and for the future, please. Join and support organizations like IMBA and COPMOBA. Pay registration fees for events like MTB Festivals. Really – trails are built not found, and that is too often via hard fighting, not a gift from Big Brother. Mountain Biking has a beautiful history. Thanks for being a part of it and supporting it. From all of us, we are honored and flattered that you, the people, have esteemed Fruita as such a key chapter in the story that is Mountain Biking.

Joe's Ridge in its early days, 1996

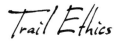

The beautiful landscapes that make up the scenery of the Grand Valley and provide the terrain for this legendary singletrack are in need of our help. Recreation is exploding – just look at all of us! With these increases come impact and damage to our environment. Or damage to our playground, as it really is. Together we can greatly reduce that impact. All it takes is just a little help from each of us.

Nature is fragile, all of it. Some of the most fragile turf is found in the high mountains and high deserts. These environments make up much of Colorado's mountain bike scene. Ongoing battles rage over how to preserve these environments for the future. Mountain bike riders need to learn how these issues affect everyone and become good stewards of the land we enjoy. By writing this I hope to help.

Environment

Sometimes those of us who recreate with machines are considered to be in opposition to environmentalists. Truth is, we who recreate outdoors obviously like the beauty of nature. Our only contest with environmentalism is the argument that the only way to save nature is to ban humans. There is a better way and that is 'use without abuse.' The way to do that is a code of conduct – ways we act that lessen our impact. We call those ethics.

Ethics

The landscapes we see are complex systems that cooperate to maintain and grow themselves. Soils are home to molds, which give start to plants, which stabilize soils for further growth. On and on it goes until these plants and animals die and even then are reused in the cycle.

So how do we ride cool trails and not wreck the very place we love? Yes, trails are paths of utter destruction. But – the good thing is that they contain all future destruction to the same area. Trails are awesome tools that allow one little path to be 'sacrificed' in order that all the surrounding earth is not. So the first and best ethic is **'stay on the trails.'** Going off-trail to by-pass an obstacle, to yield to another rider, to take a short cut or to access a trail you see across the meadow – all of this is detrimental to the soils and to the narrow tracks we love.

'**Ride don't slide.**' Skids destroy trail surface and lead to major ero-sion. Good braking doesn't skid and stops better.

'**Camp like a guest.**' Every year I have guests camp at my house for the Festival. Anyone who would cut down my trees, poop in my flowers, park on my grass or make a mess of my house will never get asked back. Get the idea? (FYI: dead and downed wood is the desert's only fertilizer.)

'**Be extra cool.**' If you want to go that extra step? Learn the 'Fruita Yield.' Yield first (since they may not know and it's really hard to discern 'uphill' here). Be really nice to everyone. Bring Troy beer/tequila and help us spread this good word to all our peers. Be an advocate. Support IMBA! (join IMBA at www.imba.com)

The Playing Field

The greatest impact I have seen from off-trail riding is by those who think they are 'fast.' I love to go fast too, and love the feeling of my wheels leaving the ground. But I ride with the mind that my tires should never leave the trail. I love singletrack as the playing field of this sport. In any sport I've played there is no provision for playing 'off the field.' The concept of being 'fast' yet unable to stay on the trail or needing to 'go around' rocks or obstacles is crazy. Riding 'the line' is our game. If we need an 'easier' or 'faster' way? Road bikes are faster and roads have far fewer obstacles. Bottom line: narrow trails are more fun anyway. Ride the trail, the way it was built; that's the playing field.

Keep Singletrack Single!

- Even when yielding, don't ride off trail; stop and step.
- Don't cut corners or go off-track to avoid bumps.
- Ride the Line! Do not ride around obstacles/rocks.
- If you happen to go 'off-trail' kick out your tracks.
- If it was 'the other guy' maybe kick out his tracks.
- Educate and set an example. We need to spread the word.

Thank You!

I·M·B·A
International Mountain
Bicycling Association
Join IMBA at **www.imba.com**

Join COPMOBA at **www.copmoba.com**

After all these years.....

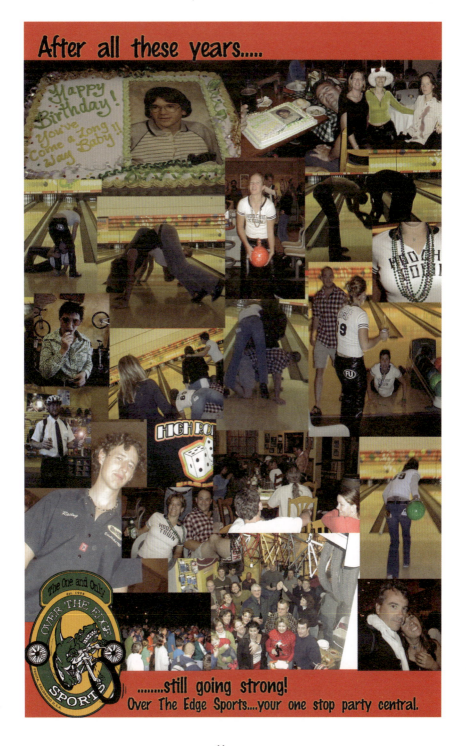

........still going strong!
Over The Edge Sports....your one stop party central.

Go-fer FOODS

CONOCO

"Fruita Freedom"
We salute your quest for freedom!

Go-fer Foods and Loma Country Store

GO-FER FOODS TWO LOCATIONS:

• On Circle Park, next to City Market.

• East on Hwy 6 & 50, next to Fruita Monument High School.

LOMA COUNTRY STORE & DELI: Beer, Gas & Food

• Downtown Loma, 5 miles west of Fruita.

Quality Conoco gasolines and diesel fuel.
Serving Fruita for over 22 years.

CASH OR CREDIT–SAME LOW PRICE

12

Kokopelli's Area Rides

KOKOPELLI'S TRAIL

The 146-mile trail from Fruita to Moab marks the beginning of Fruita Mountain Biking. The many loops off the trail near Fruita are the favorites of many mountain bikers.

In this section we will describe in detail the many loops of the Kokopelli's Trail system near Fruita. Trails here range from introductions to Fruita singletrack like Rustler's Loop to extreme technical experiences like Moore Fun. I will offer a brief overview of the entire trip from Fruita to Moab although there are entire books devoted to it. I will also mention a few 'options' for those who want to ride the entire trail but catch some 'extras' along the way.

The Kokopelli's Trail starts off the I-70 exit #15 just west of Fruita; this exit is also called the Loma exit. The Kokopelli trailhead parking lot is also the start of most of the loop rides. Additional parking is available at the Loma boat launch just south on the frontage road. This is also a good swim spot in summer.

Kokopelli's Trail

The forefathers of mountain biking in the Grand Valley had a vision – a continuous off-road trail from Fruita, Colorado to Moab, Utah. This vision founded our first MTB organization 'COPMOBA' and established a partnership with the BLM that lead to the successful completion of this trail system in the early 1990s. I wish I could pay tribute to all the folks involved but I wasn't a part of that. I do know that the Kokopelli's Trail stands as a tribute to all those who envisioned and invested all the work it takes to make a trail of such magnitude.

'Kokopelli' is a legendary figure who spread fertility to native Americans across the west. The figure of the flute-playing nomad is found in Indian art from many tribes and regions. A fitting figure for a trail that serves the day rider and the adventurer alike. Equally fitting for a trail that 'gave birth' to a mountain bike mecca in western Colorado.

KOKOPELLI'S TRAIL LOMA TO MOAB

What is it: A multi-day MTB trail on single and 2-track
Where do I start: I-70 Loma exit #15
How long: 142 miles (146 from Fruita)
Climbing: Total over 5000' / reaches over 8,000'
Highlight: Fruita singletrack and Utah desert solitude
Who rides this: MTB campers, tours and groups of intermediate & up
    ability or beginners who skip parts
Why's it cool: You won't see civilization for miles and miles
When to ride: April/May or Sept/October

Begin on fine Fruita singletrack and end on a sandy jeep road. The riding quality varies but the scenic value is ever increasing. One of the finest multi-day adventures available on a mountain bike, as well as some of the finest day rides found in each of the Kokopelli's sections.

Most commonly done as a 4-day trip. Easily supported by vehicle from easy access points. The common camping spots are: Rabbit Valley at I-70 exit #2; Overlook accessed from Westwater exit #225; Fish Ford south of Cisco UT; Dewey Bridge area, the best spots being up the gravel road to the south; Hideout being the most difficult to access; and Castle Valley, which is located in, yes, Castle Valley.

From the Loma exit / Mary's Loop parking lot: of course you start on the killer fun stuff here in Fruita. The trail uses the original Mary's and Lion's Loops and part of Troybuilt. From here you cross the Salt Wash bridge and you will not see many folks past that point. Soon singletrack gives way to 2-track and the rest of the route is scenic cruising. You pass through the heart of Rabbit Valley into Utah at about 30 miles. Overlook camp is just off Westwater exit in Utah (exit 225) and is great camping. A bit of sand takes you past the Westwater boat ramp and on to the Cisco and Fish Ford takeouts on the Colorado River. Many bypass the section before Dewey Bridge via the state highway. From Dewey you climb and then drop down a canyon and climb again, and I mean climb. Then, when you think you can't go higher than this 'polar mesa' (snow in spring), you coast down the road to Castle Valley and do it once more, finally descending Sand Flats Road into Moab.

Access points for vehicles: Rabbit Valley I-70 exit 2, Westwater (1.5 on dirt) exit Utah 225, Cisco/Fish Ford take out (6 mi south of Cisco) Dewey Bridge on Utah 128, Onion Creek with high clearance and Castle Valley / Polar Mesa off Utah 128 and all the way into Moab. Via sand flats road (dirt).

Great options for more singletrack
(Most of these are for Advanced riders)
- For a killer start do 'Moore Fun' and 'Mack Ridge' Trails
- Skip Rabbit Valley via the 'Zion Curtain'
- In Rabbit Valley use the trail #2 or the 'Western Rim'. From Overlook there is a singletrack that runs the rim towards Westwater ('Overlook trail').
- Don't skip Yellowcat...it's sandy but fun!
- Drop down Onion Creek to avoid snow on Polar Mesa.
- Finish via Porcupine Rim for an advanced finale!

Shuttle help: call Over the Edge Sports 970-858-7220
Or email: info@otesports.com

Kokopelli

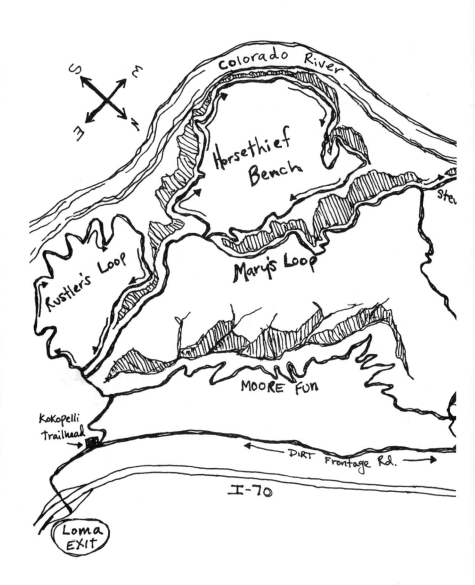

Colorado River

Horsethief Bench

Rustler's Loop

Mary's Loop

Ste...

MOORE Fun

Kokopelli
Trailhead

DIRT Frontage Rd.

I-70

Loma
EXIT

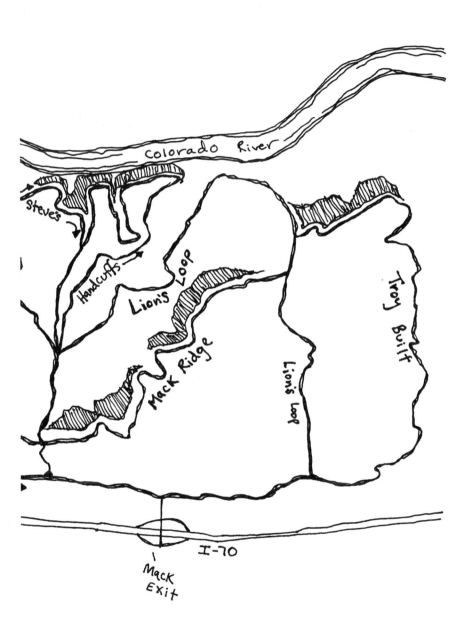

Colorado River

Steve's

Handcuffs

Lion's Loop

Mack Ridge

Lion's Loop

Troy Built

I-70

Mack Exit

Mary's Loop/Horsethief

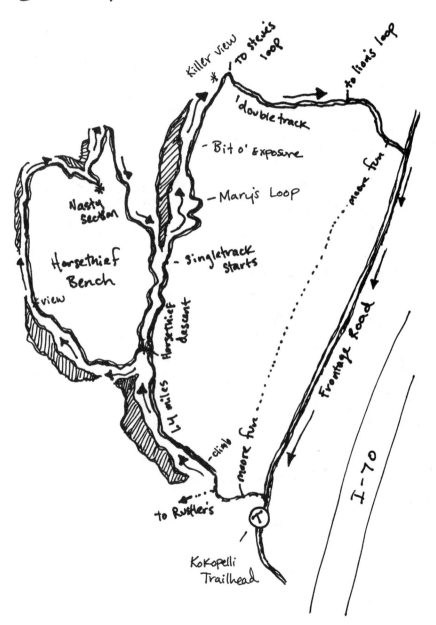

Killer view

* 'TO steve's loop

to lion's loop

'double track

- Bit o' EXPOSURE

- Mary's Loop

more fun

Nasty Section

Horsethief Bench

- singletrack starts

view

Horsethief descent

1.4 miles

more fun

Frontage Road

I-70

- climb

more fun

to Rustler's

T

Kokopelli Trailhead

Mary's Loop/Horsethief Bench

What is it: Old road to a sweet singletrack loop. A popular first ride.
Where do I start: Kokopelli's parking lot off I-70 exit 15
How long: 8-mile stem loop, including two miles up to it
Climbing: 600'
Highlight: Technical moves & ledges intermediate to daredevil (easily portaged). The best river canyon views around.
Who rides this: Everyone except novice; favorite first Fruita ride
Why's it cool: Rocks, ledges, fast & flowing
When to ride: Year round pretty much

Marked and organized by Chris Muir, this trail was built by many volunteers in minimal time. Horsethief Bench had its grand opening at the 1997 Fruita Fat Tire Festival. Although there are a couple gnarly sections, these are easily portaged.

From the parking lot, ride up the Kokopelli's on Mary's Loop. On gravel road climb over the hogback into a hidden valley. Just when you get comfortable with coasting watch for a sharp right onto a jeep trail (it's the third right after the hogback) still marked as Mary's Loop and Kokopelli's. This climbing jeep road is the final right turn just above Rustler's parking area.

Climb this jeep road and follow it along the rim with numerous views. (Remember, don't ride across the soil to get a view; many overlooks exist and off-trail travel is neither acceptable nor appreciated (see page 7). A small cattle gate to the left marks the junction with Horsethief Bench near mile 2.0 (this turn is 1.4 miles from the actual start of the Mary's double track).

Our ride turns left and descends radically down to the bench – portage! For the beginners out there, this portage does not define the rest of the trail, so don't be intimidated. For the advanced rider: this drop changes constantly, never for the better. It's very hard; I suggest a walk down first to find your best chance of survival.

At the bottom of that insane descent, please proceed left on the fine singletrack of the Bench (by keeping the traffic in one direction, we greatly reduce conflicts and trail widening).

The loop returns you back to the steep exit from the bench and back to Mary's Loop. Right returns to the start for an 8-mile trip or hang a left and complete Mary's Loop, 2.4 miles to Steve's Trail where a right turn follows the jeep road 1.7 miles back to the frontage road; turn right onto the frontage road to finish at 12.5 miles total.

Moore Fun

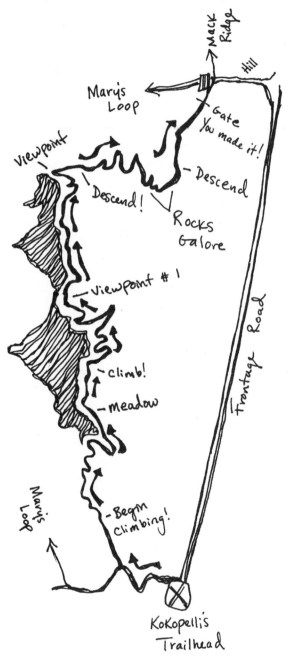

Mack Ridge

Hill

Marys Loop

Gate
You made it!

Descend

Viewpoint

Descend!

Rocks Galore

Viewpoint #1

climb!

meadow

Frontage Road

Marys Loop

Begin Climbing!

Kokopelli's Trailhead

Moore Fun

What is it: Our technical challenge singletrack. No fast air ledges, but cool tight lines on a ridgeline climb/descent
Where do I start: Kokopelli's parking lot off I-70 exit 15
How long: 9.75-mile loop with Mary's
Climbing: 950'
Highlight: Trials-type technical challenge
Who rides this: Strong rider seeking rocks, ledges, climbing
Why's it cool: Rocks! It's all ridable, but rarely all ridden
When to ride: February - November, possible year round

The Crown Jewel of Fruita to many riders. This section of the Kokopelli's System is not all that long, but you would be hard pressed to convince many of that. If this trail is over your head it can turn into a nightmare pretty quick. If you love 'trials moves' and ledge 'ups' and rock gardens this is your paradise.

Beginning from the trailhead lot you simply ride over the ridge and stay right on the singletrack that takes off as you descend the other side. The turnoff is at the apex of the left-hand corner at the bottom of the descent; if you hit the junction with Mary's Loop, you have gone too far. Once on Moore Fun there are no junctions or turn-offs. You will climb an awesome, rocky line (thanks, Kevin) to a midway park and then begin a bit more challenge up to the first high point and one great view.

After your scenic ponderings and viewings, continue on to the second summit via some really cool fast stuff and a tech finish after the 'cave' switchback. Often golden eagles are seen at this summit.

Now you're in my world. The descent brings you through some killer moves I call the 'room with a view,' the 'U-Turn' and 'the Rock'. If you haven't found a challenge by here you should turn pro. A final culminating move at the exit leads you to the saddle; Mack Ridge ahead and Mary's to the left. Finish via Mary's Loop (left) and back to the gravel road at mile 9.

Option to continue on Mack Ridge to Troy's or bail out via the frontage road to your right. If you really eat up the tech moves, climb Mack Ridge and then flip a U-turn and retrace the route. Going back is significantly harder on Moore Fun.

Enjoy...remember it's 'more fun' right?

Rustler's Loop

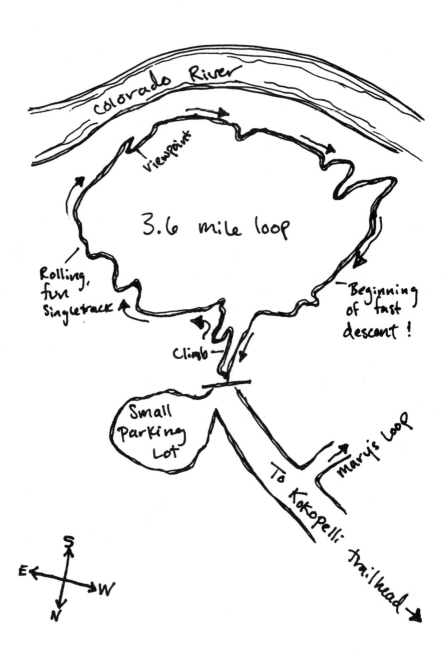

Colorado River

viewpoint

3.6 mile loop

Rolling,
fun
Singletrack

Beginning
of fast
descent !

Climb

Small
Parking
Lot

To Kokopelli Trailhead

Mary's Loop

S
E
W
N

Rustler's Loop

What is it: Easy singletrack loop for dad and brother!
Where do I start: Kokopelli's lot I-70 exit 15
How long: 3.75-mile loop
Climbing: 500'
Highlight: Fast, fun singletrack, scenic & not scary
Who rides this: Built for all and still fun for advanced
Why's it cool: Fast rhythmic flow along river views, fun for all
When to ride: Truly year round, handles wet very well

This is a great ride for anyone new to the Fruita area, or just looking for a fast singletrack loop to keep them entertained. Rustler's is 99% singletrack that is easy enough for beginners or kids but still contains enough 'smiles' for any riding ability. Beautiful views down into the Colorado and a great spot to see eagles during the winter nesting season. This loop is truly fun for everyone and a great warmup.

From the parking lot (option to drive over the hill and park at the trailhead gate) ride over the hill on gravel road all the way to the road's end at a gate. The trail begins to the right through its own gate with a big sign. The house here is private so please respect.

Once on the trail please ride 'clockwise' (to the left). You'll do a brief rocky climb and then head around a splendid twisting rolling romp on a desert bench often overlooking the spectacular Horsethief Canyon on the Colorado river. The trail finishes on a super fun twisty descent with some great 'whoops' along the way. Take the time to stop at some great overlooks or burn a hot lap and then repeat a mellow lap.

There are no turns, junctions or mileages to know. One lap is 3.75 miles and will return you to the sign, gate and start. Please respect the direction of travel as this keeps us from running into each other and thus widening this fun narrow trail.

You will notice several interpretive signs that are designed to help educate new riders about the ethics and skills of the sport. These signs were placed by COPMOBA/IMBA and have become a model around the world for rider education.

Obviously this ride can be combined in several options or used to complete the Grand Loop.

Kokopelli's area rides.
Clockwise from left:
"The Rock" on Moore
Fun; Rustler's Loop;
Horsethief Bench;
Handcuffs.

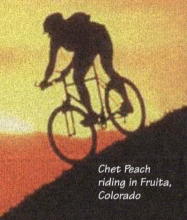

Chet Peach riding in Fruita, Colorado

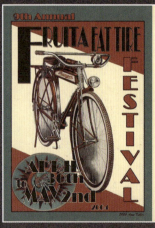

Fruita Fat Tire Festival

More fun than monkeys riding a unicycle

Last weekend in April
www.fruitamountainbike.com

Poster art by Anne Keller

The Grand Loop

What is it: Original big loop of the Kokopelli's
Where do I start: Kokopelli's lot I-70 exit 15
How long: 19.5-mile loop (25-mile option)
Climbing: 1600'
Highlight: High singletrack miles
Who rides this: Int/advanced who like long & hard
Why's it cool: Sweet singletrack variety, fast & long
When to ride: March - November (avoid when wet!)

The 'Old Man of Fruita' rides. Back in the day it was the only long ride, but it's still classic. Home of the 'Ruby Canyon Classic' race from 1993-1997.

The Loop combines Mary's, Lion's and Troy's, and returns on the frontage road. From the parking lot, ride the gravel road over the ridge, turn right in half a mile on Mary's Loop. Pass Horsethief Bench trail at two miles. Continue on Mary's Loop.

Soon the 2-track gives way to singletrack at the sign-in & map: cool singletrack above the river with a 'risky spot' near the start. Mid-way there is a plaque to Mary Nelson for whom the trail is named. This spot is one of the most photographed spots in mountain biking.

At the jeep road at 4.4 miles, make an immediate left onto Steve's trail. Drop to a junction at 5.2 miles with 'Handcuffs' and go left (or right for a shortcut*). Awesome rim one-track and jeep trail lead you back to Mary's* at 7.8 miles. Turn left to Lion's Loop junction at 8 miles; go left up Lion's Loop singletrack.

Lion's Loop is very rocky and demanding. It also has great views but you seldom look. At 10.2 miles turn right on a jeep road and climb to jct. with Troy's at 11 miles. Left on Troy's and one of my favorite descents. Superb exposed singletrack passes the Kokopelli's turn-off at 13.4 miles and continues right to the dirt road at 15 miles. This road parallels I-70 back to your start.

Option: Add a little by returning via Mary's Loop from mid-way on the road (turn right up the hill at mile 17). Or for the 'Big Loop' start on Moore Fun-Mack Ridge to Lion's Loop road; go right. At the bottom of the hill turn left on Troy's and reverse Troy's, Lion's and Mary's back to the start. (25 mi)

Mack Ridge

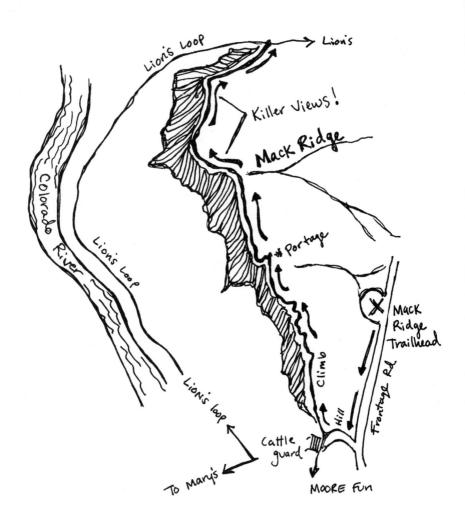

Mack began as a Tim & Troy project
and was finished in winter 99/2000
by local volunteers and an IMBA Trail
Care crew.

 **Out-n-back or as a loop with Troy Built**

What is it: Mack is a ridgeline singletrack with amazing views
Where do I start: Park just west of I-70 'Mack' exit 11
How long: 4 miles one-way Mack / 9.75-mile loop w/Troy's •
Climbing: 1100'
Highlight: Challenging trail, best views
Who rides this: Mid/upper tech skill, mid-fitness (big exposure)
Why's it cool: It's just so fun, so pretty and from Mack Ridge you overlook the entire Kokopelli's area and Colorado River canyons
When to ride: March - November; absolutely not when wet

When you don't have time for more and Horsethief Bench seems 'old & boring.' The trail works either direction; I will describe it east-to-west with the option of continuing on for a 'clockwise' loop. This affords a nice rare longish climb. If you reverse? Please yield to climbing riders!

From the Mack exit lot ride the dirt road SE (back toward Fruita) one mile; turn right onto Mary's Loop, up jeep road 1/4-mile and turn right on Mack before the cattle guard. This fine climbing singletrack makes a nice grade up the ridge reaching the top with only one portage (very rocky climb may be quite frustrating for the novice).

Up top, 2-track then 1-track run along the top of the cliff with great exposed canyon views, some of the best in the area. Meet a 2-track road at 4 miles; at this point, you can make a complete loop with Troy's, or simply turn around and retrace your route back down Mack Ridge's killer descent. Some technical sections and a billion rocks bring you back to the frontage road and a left back to the start.

To continue around Troy's for the 9.75-mile loop: from the 2-track road at 4 miles, descend to a left on Lion's Loop road; descend this cool ledgey 4x4 road to Troy's Loop (right) at 4.75 miles.

Right turn on Troy's singletrack; enjoy a splendid descent onto the bench below (remember to yield to uphill riders). The next section is so fun you'll forget the mileage, so just stay right (don't drop in/across Salt Creek) at the one intersection. A couple of climbs/descents will bring you to the road at 9 miles (stay left as you meet Lions at 9.1). Your car/start is just under 1 mile ahead. Cold beer is just 8 miles back to Fruita.

Troy Built

In spring this trail holds the best of the bloomin' cactus. Year round it is a great place to see the bright green 'collared lizard' basking.

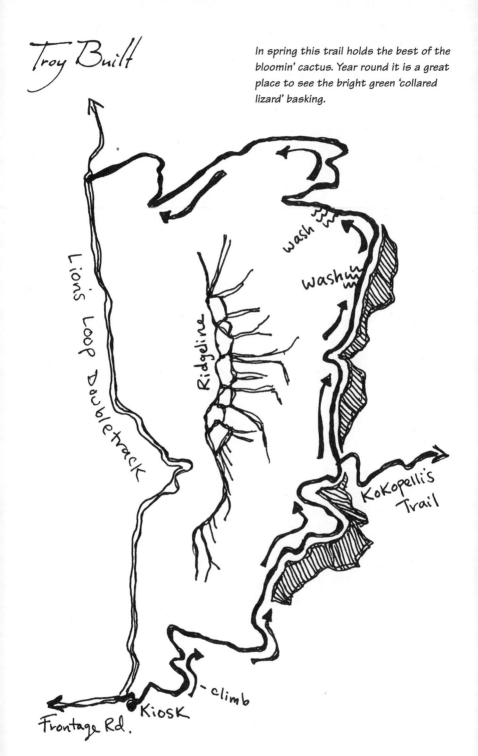

Lions Loop Doubletrack

wash

Wash

Ridgeline

Kokopelli's Trail

climb

Kiosk

Frontage Rd.

Troy Built

What is it: Technical singletrack at the north end of the Kokopelli's Loops; an out-n-back or the part of some cool loops

Where do I start: Mack exit (I-70 exit 11) parking lot

How long: 10.5-mile loop (14 w/Mack, 17 w/Handcuff)

Climbing: 950' or 2000' in the long version

Highlight: Exciting narrow rocky singletrack on a cool bench

Who rides this: Mid fitness & tech skills, likes rocks/challenge

Why's it cool: Not as popular, variety and lots of options

When to ride: March - November (Troy's is a no-go wet)

You can ride Troy's as an out-n-back and you'll ride it on a Kokopelli's trip. It's really pretty with a lot of fairly technical rock sections. The huge climb to Lion's can be avoided if you're doing the out-n-back; turn around at either the base or the top.

The basic loop is Troy Built with Lion's at 10 miles, like the Mack/Troy's ride. But I made up a combo that I found really fun, so the longer version at 14 miles is well worth checking out. This idea mixes Troy's, Lion's, back up Mack Ridge to Lion's and fast finish down Lion's screamin' jeep road descent.

From the lot 1/4 mile west of Mack exit, ride NW down the dirt road 1 mile to its end (park here for the out-n-back). Here begins Troy Built and some challenging singletrack along Salt Creek to the Colorado River. Stay left at the Kokopelli's junction at 2.3 miles. The big Troy's climb will bring you to Lion's at 5 miles (the top or the base of this monster hill is the turn-back for an out-n-back).

Breathe deep, look around, then descend right on jeep road to a quick descent to Lion's singletrack straight ahead at the switchback. The next mile is a bit rocky, be safe, have fun. A fast fun down hits Mary's/Lion's jeep road at 8.2 miles. Left here brings you to the cattle guard/Mack Ridge jct. at 9 miles. Continue down to the dirt frontage road and a left returns you to the car/start at 10.5 miles.

Option: for the longer & way fun version. Turn left & climb Mack Ridge at 9m. At the intersection with Lions jeep road at 11.7m turn right. Cross the ridge to an epic descent. Fast and rocky with pinch flat potential. You'll hit the frontage road and a right returns you to the start. (make this nearly 20 miles add in Handcuffs Loop by turning right at 8.2m and again at 8.5m)

Lion's Loop

Mary's and Lion's are the foundation of all the Kokopelli's if not Fruita mountain biking itself. Built in the early 1990's this was 'the ride' for years.

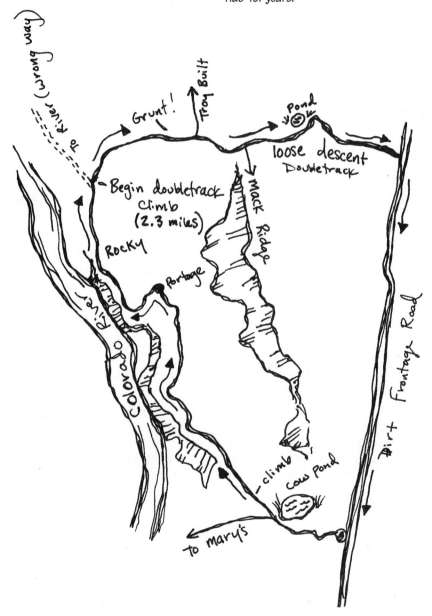

To River (wrong way)

Grunt!

Troy Built

Pond

loose descent
Doubletrack

Begin doubletrack
Climb
(2.3 miles)

Rocky

Mack Ridge

Portage

Colorado River

climb

cow pond

Dirt Frontage Road

To mary's

Lion's Loop

What is it: A Kokopelli's original 1-track & jeep road
Where do I start: Mack exit (I-70 exit 11) parking lot
How long: 6.1-mile loop (2 miles singletrack)
Climbing: 950'
Highlight: The singletrack traverse is very rocky & very cool
Who rides this: Good tech skills, or mild tech willing to walk a bit
Why's it cool: The original loop; or a great mix in with others
When to ride: February - December, maybe year round

The 'Loop' is an awesome piece of trail construction that links a bunch of jeep road. But the trail section is outstanding and justifies hanging onto its status as 'Lion's Loop.' It was also the site of the 'Ruby Canyon Classic' hosted annually by Tompkins Cycle Sports until 1997. The first known rides here were 'Mary's & Lion's.' Now Lion's is often done as a mixed-in portion of a bigger loop finishing on Troy's or Mack Ridge. But it is still worth mentioning as its own loop and is still worth doing.

From the lot 1/4 mile west of Mack exit, ride SE on the dirt frontage road 1.0 miles to a right on a climbing jeep road marked 'Lion's Loop' (parking available here). Climb over this ridge, passing Mack Ridge right and Moore Fun left at 1.1 miles; stay right on the jeep road and turn right onto climbing singletrack at 1.5 miles.

Singletrack begins with a stiff climb then becomes intermittently fast and rocky, eventually rock traverse wins out on the Lion's highlight section. Great moves and big exposure make this forever a classic. When you hit the jeep road at 3.8 miles, climb right (left descends to private property) and pass Troy's left at 4.5 miles. Right after the top of the climb Mack Ridge will go right on a 2-track; Lion's stays left across the top of the mesa like ridgetop. One final little left-bending climb by a pond leads to the bomber descent down — the fastest all-out descent on Kokopelli's. Hopefully before you pinch flat you reach the dirt frontage road at 5.5 miles (Troy Built to the left), and a right turn back to the start at 6.1 miles.

Obviously this fits easily into many contrived loop options and I'll leave that to your imagination. Yes, every section of Lion's gets ridden, both ways. The middle rock move is quite a trophy and I would say Lion's wins the majority of the challenges.

Handcuffs / Steve's Loop

What is it: A short fun singletrack loop to combine with other rides or a scenic mini ride by itself
Where do I start: Park 1mile South of Mack exit #11
How long: 5-mile loop & back
Climbing: 400'
Highlight: Narrow track along the canyon rim
Who rides this: Intermediate or careful novice, low tech
Why's it cool: Winds along the cliffs above the river...so romantic
When to ride: February - November

The loop was built by Fruita locals in the mid 90s. Steve's is the connector to Mary's Loop, built in 1998, thanks Foote/Rusk. The Handcuffs part runs the canyon rim so close to the edge it's a bit tense at times. But the scenic value is outstanding and worth a look. It has a bit of technical (ridden both ways) but is doable and rewarding for the careful novice. Please help keep it narrow — no shortcuts, new overlooks, or off-trail riding — it's in very fragile soils.

Of course you can add this to anything that comes by way of Mary's Loop (turn toward the river as you come up to the jeep road viewpoint) or Lion's/Moore Fun (turn right just past the Lion's Loop singletrack) or use half this trail as a way to avoid the Mary's Loop road.

As its own ride this is a great sunset cruise or intro to 'harder' trails for the novice. Park in the turn-out one mile south of Mack exit on the dirt road. Ride over the hill away from I-70 on Mary's loop 2-track, passing Mack Ridge at the top. Continue, now descending, immediately passing a jeep road left, then Lion's Loop on the right (optional trail parallels the road here) and take the very next right at about 1 mile. Ride this old 2-track to the very end and descend a singletrack toward the river. Stay left as a tempting right goes nowhere. Enjoy this narrow trail (it's OK to walk) around several small side canyons with great river views to the slickrock wash and junction with Steve's at 3.4 miles.

Continue left .4 miles to a short hike-a-bike leading back to (previous mile 1) Mary's Loop road. Re-trace the 2-track, now a gradual climb, past Lion's, Moore Fun and Mack ridge back to the start at 5 miles.

The Tunnel

What is it: A big loop using pavement, dirt road to a return via
Kokopelli's Trail to Fruita / Loma
Where do I start: Over the Edge, downtown Fruita
How long: 41-mile loop
Climbing: 2600'
Highlight: Big miles, no shuttle
Who rides this: Mid+ tech skills with huge fitness
Why's it cool: Ride from town, finish on great 1-track
When to ride: March - November

This is big! Riding from Fruita, returning on Kokopelli's singletrack, with
much hard riding. May be shortened 10 miles by parking at Loma
Country Store, or lengthened by adding optional Loops. Yeah, right.

Head west on Aspen Avenue, blending into old US6; continue west
through Loma and Mack. Turn left off pavement onto a dirt road atop a
small rise, 5.7 miles past Mack store (1.7 past stone bridge/mm12).
Cross a cattle guard and make a sharp left. This is the road that will
take you under I-70 via a small tunnel and meet the Kokopelli's trail
(still a dirt road) at 17.5 miles. Turn left just through the tunnel and
stay left again at junction.

Go left (eastbound) on the Kokopelli's, still on dirt road. The route
from here should be well marked. There is a great overlook to the right at
19.7 miles. Our route continues on to a right on singletrack at 20 miles.
Now we are on our well-deserved reward: wonderful Fruita singletrack!

Great riding down into Salt Creek. Watch the ruts and beware the
big drops just before the railroad. After passing under the bridge and
crossing Salt Creek, a short climb and carry brings you to Troy's Loop
at 22.5 miles. Turn right on this fine track until an epic climb brings you
to Lion's Loop at 25 miles. Right again (or left to a Mack Ridge option)
and continue Lion's to the Mary's Junction at 28 miles.

Right again on Mary's, passing Steve's at 28.2 (option #2) and
Horsethief Bench at 31.7 mile. (option #3). Complete Mary's loop 2-track
to left turn on gravel 33 miles to right turn on frontage road and the
I-70 exit #19 at 35 miles. Cross I-70 and descend to Loma and US6 at
37 miles. A right will bring you back to Fruita and a weary 41 miles.

Parking at Loma store will take a solid 10 miles off this ride and
they have cold drinks; net distance 31.7 miles.

Rides

THE BOOKCLIFF TRAILS

This trail system was the true original creation of Fruita mountain bikers and was also the point where Fruita changed from a local secret to a national destination.

Many claimed we had the first Fruita Fat Tire Festival in 1996 as a way to help 'pack in' the new trails we built in the Bookcliffs area off 18 Road (I'll never tell). People came and people talked. Magazine writers and cycling legends talked about the magic of Fruita and thus a destination was born.

Fast, twisting and full of surprises — built entirely by and for mountain bikes, these trails are special. The magic still lives and in the Bookcliffs, you can feel it.

The Bookcliffs

'Bookcliffs' is the name of the dominant cliffs that form the northern border of the Grand Valley. This 'ancient shoreline' of sandstone and adobe runs far into Utah. The Bookcliffs, now known for MTB trails, are laced with coal seams and home to the infamous oil shale naval energy reserve project of the 1980s that, in it's abandonment (1982) nearly bankrupt several towns of western Colorado.

Years ago filmmakers showed riders skidding down these adobe hills. Things have changed much since then as that portion of the Bookcliffs is now closed off and narrow singletrack with good trail ethics is the area theme. Just so you know: we certainly do not do that here. Off-trail riding is not what makes free-riding. Please stay on trails; thanks.

Over the Edge Sports was established in downtown Fruita in 1995. That same year the Bookcliffs trail system north of Fruita was born. Fruita and 'Edge' locals devoted thousands of hours to developing routes and constructing these trails off 18 Road. Tom, Joe, Scott, Doug, Carl, John, Gary, Brian, Kevin, Sarah, Jen, Kurt, myself and many more devoted years to developing one of the finest collections of singletrack found, still one of the few trail systems anywhere designed and built by mountain bikers for mountain bikers. We are proud of these trails and the accolades they have received.

ACCESS/DIRECTIONS From Over the Edge / downtown Fruita

To The Bookcliffs/18 Road East on Aspen Ave (away from circle park). Left on Maple (2nd stop sign). Continue north on Maple (17.5 Rd.) 3.8 miles, turn right on N 3/10 Rd. (paved turn lane). T into 18 Rd., go left, once on dirt (stay left on the main road at the various forks); continue 4.3 miles to parking area on the left.

Hunters/21 Road Drive north from the circle park to 'Ottley' Drive; east on Ottley (K Rd.) to 21 Rd. Go north on 21 Rd. to dirt; continue several miles to a fork; continue straight ahead (right fork) to hunters parking across the small wash.

Via 16 Road West on Aspen; join Hwy 6 & turn north (right) on 16 Rd., 12.7 mi. (half on dirt); park at a junction.

Douglas Pass 5 miles west on Hwy 6 to Loma, turn right on Hwy 139; go north of Loma 30 miles. Park at the top of Douglas Pass.

Edge Loop

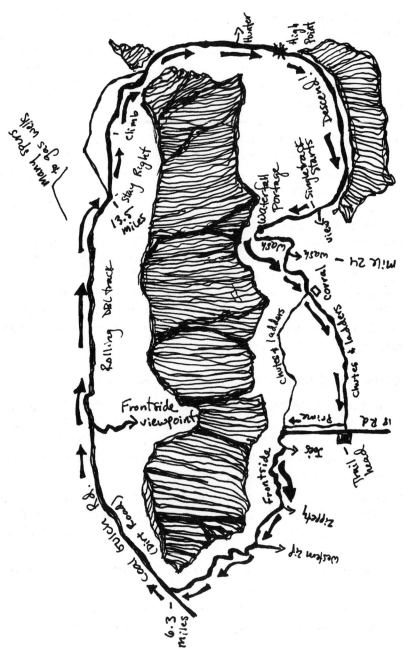

→ Hunter

High Point

Descending

Climb

stay Right

13.5 miles

many spots at gas wells

Rolling DBL track

Frontside viewpoint

Coal Gulch Rd. (dirt Road)

6.3 miles

Singletrack starts

Waterfall Portage

views

450m Wash

Mile 24

Corral

Chutes & ladders

Chutes & ladders

Bridge

15 Rd

Trail Head

Frontside

Sees

zippety

Western zip

The Edge Loop

Fruita's Flagship / IMBA's first Epic ride

What is it: Acclaimed as one of the best MTB rides in the country.
A true loop, start/finish on singletrack. No escape, very fun!

Where do I start: Bookcliffs parking lot (see previous page)

How long: 29.2-mile loop, feels like 35. Average ride times are from a
fastest time of <3 hours to an epic of 7. (7,326' high pt.)

Climbing: 3200'

Highlight: The final 11 miles, so sweet!

Who rides this: 'You gotta ride it' mid technical/strong effort

Why's it cool: So remote, so scenic, such good riding, so big

When to ride: April - September (October is hunting season)

The Edge Loop was conceived early on in Fruita history. Scouted in 1995
and completed in 1996, it still stands as one of the greatest achieve-
ments of Fruita's band of trail builders. To the visionaries of 18 Road,
this is our true love. The completion of this loop holds volumes of sto-
ries: Scott and Tom's overnight recon trips; Troy and Loren's airplane
scouting and the excitement in its completion. This trail is the crown of
Fruita, site of the very first IMBA Epic Ride, and one BIG ride. Much of
this trail is on 'the edge,' thus the name. From the top the view of the
Grand Valley is spectacular, reaching from the San Juan mountains to
the south and the La Sals of Moab to the southwest.

Be really prepared for this, it's big, it's remote and be aware, there
is no retreat from this loop. It can snow up top. That being said, it's so
well worth the endeavor that most people who ride in Fruita for long
make certain they get this one under the belt. It's so good that you
want to be able to say 'I rode the Edge Loop.' I have tweaked the route
slightly since the original in light of the expansion of the Bookcliffs Trail
system and some new options. So, here is the suggested route...

From 18 Road parking lot: you can start the loop any number of
ways as long as you get on the 'Frontside' trail. Originally the route
started up Prime Cut from the parking lot, left at Chutes jct. across 18
Road at top, right on Joes/Frontside/Edge trail. (mi 2.4), continuing out
the Frontside trail to the meadow at mile 5. This is the way that it is
drawn on the corresponding map.

Now I might suggest heading west out of the back corner of the
parking lot, stay left when you hit Zippety (.75) and then right on the
Zip 2-track (1.3) and up the western Zippety singletrack (right at 3).
This way or the aforementioned way will bring you to the western

Zip/Frontside intersection in a meadow at mile 5 (either way).

From the 5-mile meadow intersection, continue out the Frontside singletrack to a right on Coal Gulch Road at 6.3 mile. Enjoy this fire road for a while; stay right and climb at 13.5 miles! Follow main road up – long climb, great views – to ridgetop meadow at 16 miles. Follow ridgetop road south; do not descend off either side. The road passes many spurs and gas wells; one has a pump motor always running to let you know you're on track.

Pass Hunter's Canyon 4-way at 17.5 miles, keep straight ahead, staying on the ridge line. Pass the last gas well, through an old gate and suddenly the road reverts to barely 2-track. This is the high point, 7326 feet, at 18 miles. Now old 2-track rolling with fast descents and one short wall climb. Just after the small climbs at the top of the first huge downhill, there is a great viewpoint left and a good stopping place at 19.5 mile. This downhill is the first of three very steep descents with surreal views. After the third steep down there is a right turn onto singletrack at the top of the next small crest at 21 mile.

Turn right on the trail away from the spectacular views of the Grand Valley. This is getting good now! Descend like a giggling schoolgirl into the canyon below, turn left in the wash. Sorry about the sand and weeds. You'll know when you reach the portage, a 30' waterfall, at mile 22.5. Be careful, use teamwork. There is usually a rope. Please don't make bypass trails (there is some discussion about the BLM building a bypass, of course there is discussion about opening the trail to MOTO use as well. We hope when you get here you still get the fun of descending the waterfall. I always will). This is the infamous Edge Loop waterfall and although it seems dramatic, no one has ever been hurt here. Let's keep it that way. Once you're down, swap tales and continue down the wash. Ride the wash .5 miles and watch for the trail that stays out of creek bed, saving you from a sandy fate. This trail crosses the wash several times; be aware of washed-out transitions. Leave the wash at 24 miles for the final time, crossing a grassy meadow on singletrack to a challenging up.

Singletrack heads west as you leave the canyon. Three challenging climbs keep you working. With a final rousing descent to a road at 26 miles. Left on this 2-Track road for just one mile to right turn onto 'abused' one-track heading to a diamond-fenced corral off to your right (27). At the corral (you are now on the final leg of the 'Chutes and Ladders' trail) make a left along fence for a fast singletrack across the desert where a steep climb and the final short climb up from the Prime Cut stock tank brings you back to the start at mile 29.2. You have now done 'The Edge Loop!'

SURLY®

www.surlybikes.com
1-877-743-3191

Bookcliffs

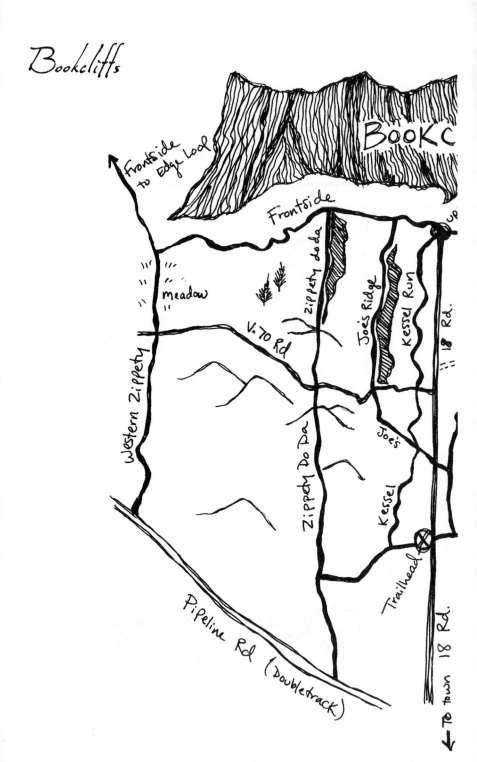

Frontside to Edge Loop

BookC

Frontside

meadow

Zippety doda

Joe's Ridge

Kessel Run

up

18 Rd.

V. To Rd

Western Zippety

Zippety Do Da

Joe's

Kessel

Trailhead

Pipeline Rd (Doubletrack)

To town 18 Rd.

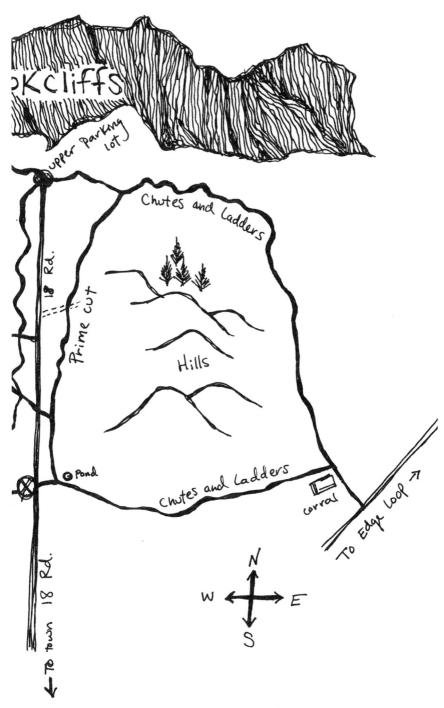

Kcliffs

upper parking lot

Chutes and Ladders

18 Rd.

Prime cut

Hills

Pond

Chutes and Ladders

corral

To Edge Loop ↗

To town 18 Rd.

N
W ←→ E
S

43

Prime Cut / Joe's Ridge

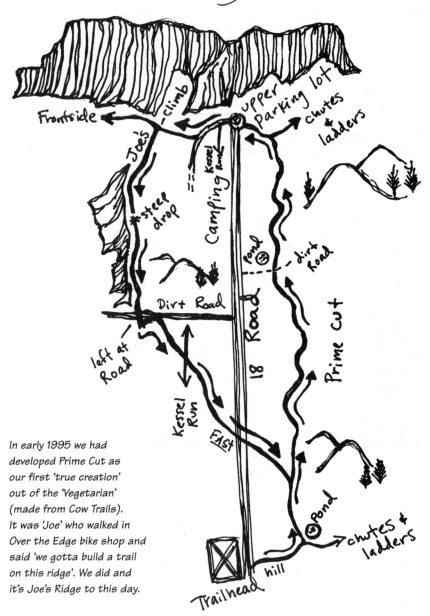

Frontside ← --climb-- upper parking lot chutes & ladders

Joe's Kessel Run Camping pond ⓢ dirt Road

*steep drop

Dirt Road

18 Road

Prime Cut

left at Road

Kessel Run

Fast

pond ⓢ chutes & ladders

hill

Trailhead

In early 1995 we had developed Prime Cut as our first 'true creation' out of the 'Vegetarian' (made from Cow Trails). It was 'Joe' who walked in Over the Edge bike shop and said 'we gotta build a trail on this ridge'. We did and it's Joe's Ridge to this day.

Prime Cut / Joe's Ridge

What is it: The original Bookcliffs Loop, short and still fun
Where do I start: Bookcliffs / 18 Road parking lot
How Long: 5.5-mile loop
Climbing: 450'
Highlight: Joe's BIG descent and no climbing, well...
Who rides this: Int/novice singletrack lover seeking short loop
Why's it cool: 99% sweet singletrack, an MTB legend
When to ride: February - November (no go when wet)

The beginning and still the core of Bookcliff/18 Road trails. Not the longest, not the hardest and maybe not the best. But Joe's was one of the first and is a very good ride. Most of all, Joe's Ridge epitomizes Fruita: the vision of trails by and for MTB experience. It's development is a tribute to the people who made Fruita happen.

From the parking lot 4.3 miles past the end of pavement on 18 Road, cross the road and drop to the cow pond; a left turn and you're climbing up the small valley of Prime Cut. Follow this all the way up to the base of the hills and Chutes jct at 1.9 miles. Stay left here and (stay right on the camp road) meet the top of 18 Road at 2.2 miles.

Cross 18 Road and descend on 2-track camping road turning right on singletrack in only 200 yards (easy to miss). Climb slightly again on this one-track to a switchback left turn at 2.5 miles just after the rocky wash (Frontside continues straight ahead). Immediately you descend through a fast, twisty, delightful meadow. A short climb up a skinny ridge brings you to the namesake descent. This wild ride is a hoot for the advanced, a test for the veteran, and a short walk for the nervous. At the base of the descent lie several rock pile 'kickers' that have gained a reputation for pitching folks over the bars. Jump em' well, or watch your speed coming into these. A mini climb brings you to a 2-track, then road at 3.6 miles.

Left on this road and a right on a singletrack just after the wash brings you to Kessell Run (right in .5 miles) or back to 18 Road in 1.1 miles. Right on the road gets you back or cross the road and drop back into Prime Cut. Either way you will be back at the car and a nice finish at mile 5.5.

Joe's makes a great combo with other rides and has even been climbed. Joe's was also the photo in Fruita's first magazine appearance: Bicycling Magazine, Sept. 1995. Joe's Ridge has been immortalized in a wonderful video by Pete Fagerlin (www.petefagerlin.com).

Kessel Run

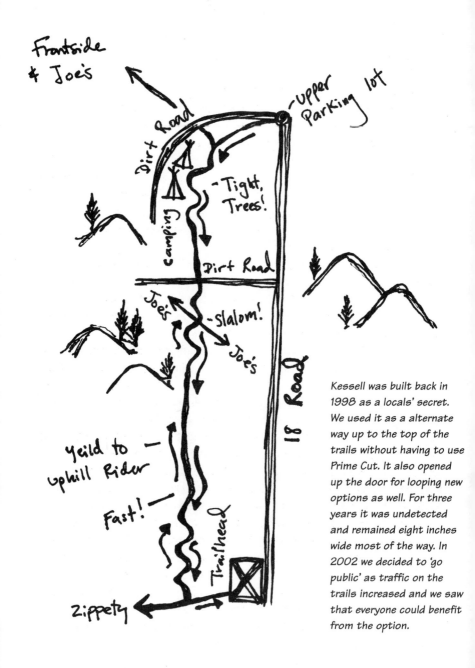

Frontside & Joe's

Upper Parking lot

Dirt Road

Tight, Trees!

camping

Dirt Road

Joe's

Slalom!

Joe's

18 Road

Yeild to uphill Rider

Fast!

Trailhead

Zippety

Kessell was built back in 1998 as a locals' secret. We used it as a alternate way up to the top of the trails without having to use Prime Cut. It also opened up the door for looping new options as well. For three years it was undetected and remained eight inches wide most of the way. In 2002 we decided to 'go public' as traffic on the trails increased and we saw that everyone could benefit from the option.

Kessell Run

What is it: The other trail that parallels 18 Road
Where do I start: Bookcliffs/18 Road parking lot for the climbing version,
    the top of 18 Road for the descent
How long: 2.2 miles
Climbing: 300'
Highlight: A virtual singletrack slalom course
Who rides this: Those looking for a good time not a straight line
Why's it cool: Fast turns, jumps, always twisting...entertaining
When to ride: Year round, avoid when wet, please...really

To the credit of our MTB guests, Kessell has gotten wider but not by
much. It's the 'Fruita way' to keep this trail narrow and fun. If the line
goes over the rock? We meant for it to; please don't ride around it.
Please 'Ride the Line.' Thanks and enjoy.

For the climbing version, ride out the back corner of the parking lot,
descend that first hill and Kessell Run goes right from the bottom (.2
mile). From here Kessell winds back and forth, up and down up this
drainage. It crosses lower Joe's Ridge at 1 mile and crosses the gravel
road at 1.25 miles. The trail continues across the road and winds still
up to an intersection at 2 miles. This intersection leads left to the top
of Joe's Ridge or right to the top of 18 Road and Prime Cut / Chutes &
Ladders.

Turn around here to make an out-and-back or use this as access to
most of the rest of the Bookcliffs trails.

Note: *You will see occasional trails develop from campsites to Kessell or
from the back side of the fenced corral at mile 1.4 over to 18 Road/Prime.
These are ridiculous. I hope you will help us in educating the folks
who make these trails. If everyone needs a trail from their car to the
singletrack there won't be any more singletrack. The mentality of this is
utterly selfish and short-sighted. From smack dab in the middle of the
camping area it is a whopping half mile to any trail head. We the locals
have worked in the dirt and in the political circle to build, maintain and
defend this area for all of us to enjoy. 30,000 people a year come to
enjoy it; none of us come to destroy it.*

Chutes & Ladders

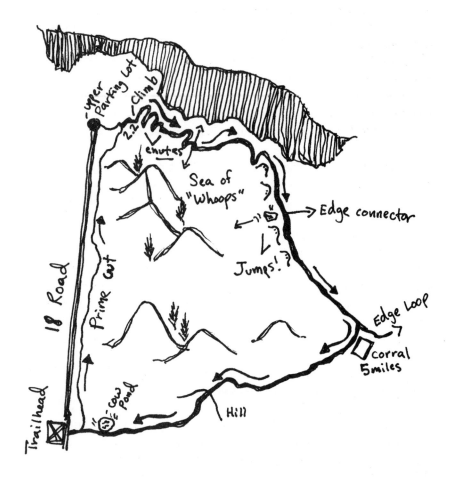

'Chutes & Ladders' consistently challenges all riding skills. Rarely does anyone clean all of 'Chutes'. This trail was built by the author with his 3 year old son Jordan in the fall of 1995 and became the second loop on 18 road. The game "Chutes and Ladders" and the steep ups and downs of the trail fit so perfectly it was a natural fit for the name.

Chutes and Ladders

What is it: 100% singletrack, challenge, hoots & hollers!
Where do I start: Bookcliffs / 18 Road parking lot
How long: 7-mile loop (ride clockwise)
Climbing: 500' in several short and steep challenges
Highlight: Descending steep chutes and climbing steep ladders
Who rides this: Low-tech, mid fitness, hard steep sections
Why's it cool: Easy up, hairy namesake hill section, fast finish...jumps!
When to ride: February - November (no go when wet)

Cross the road from the parking lot. Drop to the cow pond and left on singletrack up a small valley on 'Prime Cut.' Singletrack climbs in a beautiful drainage to another cow pond at 1 mile. Continue to climb gradually through scrub juniper forest, twisting and turning across many small drainages. Near the base of the Bookcliffs, at mile 2, turn right up 'Chutes and Ladders.'

The 'Chutes & Ladders' begin in earnest with three steep climbs, or 'ladders.' The next mile holds many steep climbs and descents, so steep they are often walked (if you hate the start...reconsider). Cross a wash and climb to an old 2-track at 3 miles make an obvious, quick, left on singletrack.

The trail changes here and picks up speed with little climbing remaining. Cross another old 2-track at 3.5 miles and descend through a meadow known as the 'grassy knoll.' Pass an old pond at 4 miles; singletrack stays left along a small dam (you might notice the Edge/Chutes connector going left here). What comes next is the favorite of many who ride Chutes. Very fast and fun, 'feels like dual slalom' with many jumps, fast turns and giggles. You hit the 'corral' intersection at mile 5.

Turn right along the fence on big ring one-track heading west. Rip down a big wash and climb one last ridge, arriving back at the cow pond just below the parking lot at mile 6.8; up the hill and you're back to the start.

Please note: sometimes the cows make the trail bumpy. If we all ride on those bumps we will smooth them out. If we ride next to them we will make it a 2-track.

The Frontside

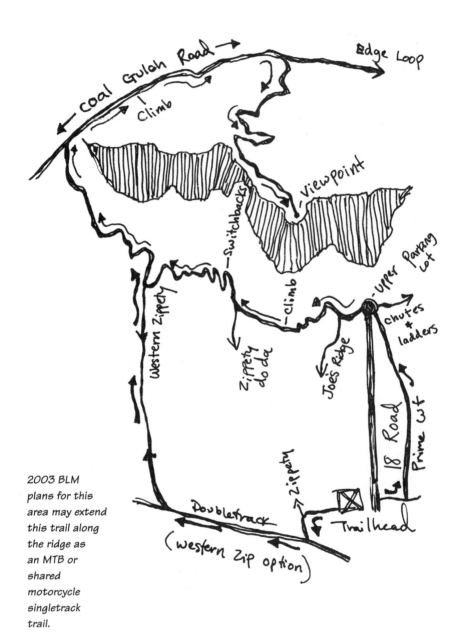

Coal Gulch Road →

Edge Loop

Climb

viewpoint

Switchbacks

Climb

Western Zippety

Zippety do da

Joe's Ridge

Upper Parking Lot

chutes + ladders

18 Road

Prime cut

Zippety

Doubletrack

(western Zip option)

Trailhead

2003 BLM plans for this area may extend this trail along the ridge as an MTB or shared motorcycle singletrack trail.

The Frontside

What is it: Singletrack to the top of the Bookcliffs, via the 'Frontside.'
Where do I start: Bookcliffs / 18 road parking lot
How long: 10.5 miles each way / 21 miles round trip
Climbing: 1700' top at 6400' one great climb
Who rides this: Low tech, mid-upper fitness, wow views.
Why's it cool: Climb to elevation and a cool destination
When to ride: April - October

Ninety percent singletrack to the best climb in the area. In 1995 Troy and his father flew recon missions in a Cessna 172 for what became 'The Edge Loop.' The Frontside was born out of an old coal mine road that showed up in these aerial photos. Combined with the 1996 singletrack start to the Edge Loop an awesome ride was born. In 1997 we rode Frontside as a loop descending the front of the Bookcliffs. Since then erosion, private property and sheer steepness has made that loop obsolete (a bad hike).

From the 18 Road lot start up Prime Cut across the road, left at 2.2 miles across 18 Road and right onto Frontside/Joe's Ridge single-track. Stay right at Joe's Ridge, mile 2.5, and enjoy the fabulous fast singletrack across the Frontside to the Zippety Ridge at 4 miles. One good climb and a rousing switchback descent brings you to 'the meadow' intersection at 5 miles.

From 'the meadow' continue out the Frontside (uphill/west) single-track to Coal Gulch road at mile 6.3, turn right on road. Ride up road for 2.1 miles to a hidden right turn onto singletrack/old road at 8.4 miles (this turn-off sits to the right on a left bend in the road at a small canyon mouth). A wonderful multi-gear climb with some steep pitches, rest sections and tremendous views. After the final steep pitch reach the viewpoint summit at 10.5 miles, 1500' above your starting point directly below.

Retrace your route to the meadow at previous mile 5, stay left on Frontside for two miles and descend Joe's Ridge, Kessell or Prime Cut; all of which descend to the start. Zippety, the ridge top right after the switchbacks, is very advanced.

Zippety Do Da

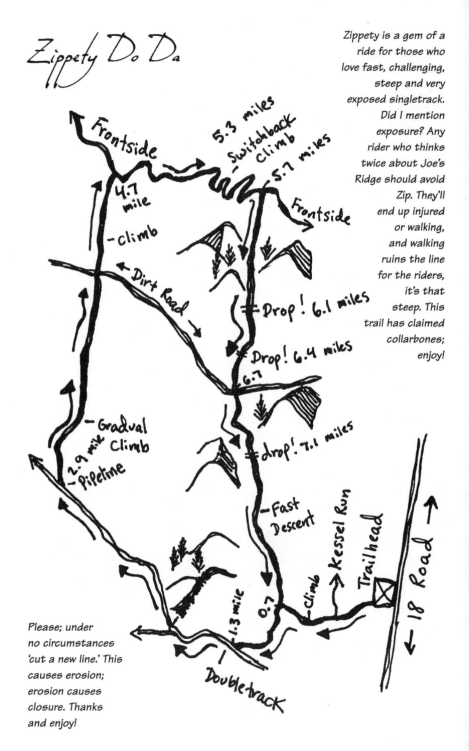

Zippety is a gem of a ride for those who love fast, challenging, steep and very exposed singletrack. Did I mention exposure? Any rider who thinks twice about Joe's Ridge should avoid Zip. They'll end up injured or walking, and walking ruins the line for the riders, it's that steep. This trail has claimed collarbones; enjoy!

Frontside

5.3 miles
Switchback Climb

5.7 miles

Frontside

4.7 mile

- climb

← Dirt Road →

＝ Drop! 6.1 miles

＝ Drop! 6.4 miles

6.7

＝ drop! 7.1 miles

- Gradual Climb
2.9 mile
- Pipeline

- Fast Descent

1.3 mile

0.7

- Climb

→ Kessel Run

Trailhead

← 18 Road →

Doubletrack

Please; under no circumstances 'cut a new line.' This causes erosion; erosion causes closure. Thanks and enjoy!

52

Zippety Do Da

What is it: Steep daring ridgeline challenge or lame hike
Where do I start: Bookcliffs / 18 road parking lot
How long: 8.8-mile loop (ride clockwise)
Climbing: 700' (one whopper set of switchbacks)
Highlight: The thrill of that first descent never fades
Who rides this: Skilled rider seeking good time with thrilling steeps
Why's it cool: Mellow start, leads to a 'pucker factor' wild finish
When to ride: March - November (no go when wet)

Nice mellow start leads to the hardest climb on 18 Road and the steepest descents. Built by the author and Wayne Petefish in 1996, Zip was made to give skilled riders a place to drop steeps without riding off trail. The BLM has been awesome in supporting such a trail. Unfortunately some have bypassed the steep sections and made new lines. Don't! This ruins a great trail. Please...ride the line.

Head west from the parking lot. Pass Kessell Run, cross a cattle guard and climb to a left at 0.8 miles, right on 2-track at 1.4 (keep right at power line), right on 1-track at 3 miles. Climbing gradually you cross a fence then a road (4.5), reaching Frontside jct, in a lovely meadow. At 5 miles. turn right.

Fast-rolling one-track along the base of the Bookcliffs brings you to 'the switchbacks' at 5.4 miles, a huge challenge to clear this hill, dig deep! Now on the ridgeline, watch for a trail right, staying on the ridgeline, at 5.7 where 'Frontside' goes left. Stay right, on the ridge; this is where Zip gets hard.

A nice scenic narrow ridge run begins to descend left at 6.1 miles, suddenly the trail turns hard left, drops a big rock step into a steep downhill. 'My oh my what a wonderful day.' Some air this, most carefully roll it, but please don't make a way around it.

Fast fun ridge rollers, a steep climb up the 'tight rope' to another hard left into another fun, fast, steep drop brings you to the road at 6.7 mile. Cross the road and climb back up to the ridge. A third big drop at mile 7.1 has a bypass left. One last extreme steep climb up the ridge and a quick cruise to the junction at 8.1 (previous mile 0.8) where a left returns you to the start.

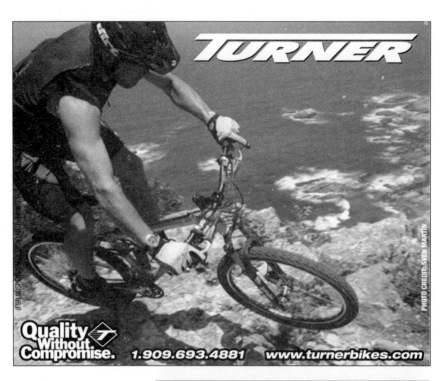

Bookcliffs
singletrack

The Perimeter

What is it: Super varied, combines Western Zip, Frontside, and Chutes.
Where do I start: Bookcliffs / 18 road parking lot
How long: 12-mile loop (ride clockwise)
Climbing: 950' (mostly in short/steep segments)
Highlight: The full tour of the Bookcliff trails
Who rides this: Mid fitness, mild tech skills with some hard climbs
Why's it cool: Variety & length; hard climbs, fast downs
When to ride: March - November (no go when wet)

So named because it skirts the perimeter of the core Bookcliffs singletracks and is a great introduction to the area. Twelve miles, 90% singletrack, with options to make it 20 miles. The speed, challenges and quality of this ride make it one of the locals favorites. Miles of high speed singletrack will entertain you as much as the steep climbs of Chutes and Frontside switchbacks will challenge you.

Start as for Zip, west from lot, left at 0.8, right at 1.4 (on the only 2-track) and right on singletrack at 3 miles. Climb one-track to Frontside meadow and a right at 5 miles. Heading east along the base of the Bookcliffs you encounter 'the switchbacks' at 5.4 and stay left at the Zippety turn-off at 5.7 miles. Cool singletrack climbs and descents bring you past Joe's Ridge and back to 18 Road at 7 mile. Stay left at 2-track, cross 18 Road and turn left back on Prime Cut singletrack, heading east along the base of the hills.

Climb left on Chutes & Ladders at 7.5 (marked with a post/two very steep climbs right away), staying close to the base of the hills. Now on Chutes the theme is steep ups and downs. Challenge yourself, walk if you must; it only lasts for a mile or so. Obvious singletrack crosses old roads and begins to descend. Fast and narrow cruising across the 'grassy knoll' leads away from the Bookcliffs towards the valley. Stay right at the old cow pond following the singletrack left along the dam. The next section, known as the 'sea of woops,' feels like a clinic in flow with 'air' potential in abundance (keep it narrow, don't leave the trail, ride the line!).

The trail joins a road momentarily to a junction at the Corral at mile 10.4; turn right along the fence and cruise fast one-track due west toward the start. This big ring reward continues for several miles to finish a great ride. One small climb ends the speed session and brings you in sight of the climb to the parking lot and final climb to the finish at mile 12.2

Add the rest of the Frontside or a visit to the Edge Loop and you can easily add 10-plus miles to this loop.

Chet Peach Memorial Race Course

RIDING FROM THE PAVEMENT END TO TRAILS

What is it: The Bookcliffs XC race course or a ride out to trails
Where do I start: 18 Road turns to dirt; go right 1 mile to start
How long: 5.6 miles to Prime Cut Pond / 22-mile course
Climbing: 300'
Who rides this: Those in the race or want more mileage
Why's it cool: Why drive out when you can ride out?
When to ride: Year round sans wet

The Race Course constantly varies due to being destroyed by XC redneck travel, but hopefully the 2004 BLM plan will include this as a protected route. This description will get you started on the course or help you ride out to the Prime Cut pond. The full race course may be marked in spring and obscure by fall.

From the end of the pavement take the right fork in the road and drive 2.0 miles to park at gas line jct. (or to ride from pavement end...head up and east till you find yourself paralleling a fence; don't cross the cattle guard; stay along this fence on a 2-track north, through a gate at 1.5mile; meet the gas line road; a left will bring you to the S/F line).

The race course begins out the gas line 2-track; to ride out to trails find the singletrack just east of the S/F parking. Once on this single-track (may be barely used), head due north, cross a road, stay straight on cow trail till you cross dirt road (left); pass a cow pond (stay right) and climb on 1-track, crossing a road at the top. Go straight across, descend fun singletrack, cross one more 2-track, continue north to Prime Cut cow pond just below the parking lot at mile 5.6.

Proud sponsor of the Fruita Fat Tire Festival

The Edge Out & Back

What is it: Scenic singletrack on the awesome Edge Loop
Where do I start: Bookcliffs / 18 Road parking lot
How long: 16 miles out & back
Climbing: 1800' (600 to portage & back)
Highlights: Some of the purest singletrack known to man
Who rides this: Adventurous, skilled riders w/good fitness
Why's it cool: Remote, narrow, scenic and different
When to ride: Late February - November (no go when wet)

This is a great out-and-back ride for the adventurer and an early season version of the Edge Loop. Riding the best of the Edge Loop singletrack, this explores remote areas of the Bookcliffs and has stayed extremely narrow thanks to the skill and care of Edge Loop riders. Thanks for carrying on that tradition.

Begin on singletrack across the road from the parking lot. Stay right across the cow pond dam, heading east on Chutes singletrack. At the corral at 1.8 miles, turn right (east) to a road at 2.1 miles. Turn left up this 2-track, keep right at 2.8, climbing toward Layton Canyon, to a trail right at 3.2 miles.

Turn right onto singletrack, cross a wash and up a short climb. Wonderful rolling trail, mostly less than a foot wide, brings you to Lipan Canyon at 5 miles where the trail heads up into the canyon. This section was built for the festival in 1998, a huge improvement over the sandy wash. The trail returns to the wash and brings you to the famous waterfall at 6.5 miles. You can turn around here for a shortened version or climb on up to the rim overlook.

To continue, climb the waterfall and ride up the wash. In a half mile the trail will leave the wash to the right and begin a real climb. A very steep start meets an old dozer cut and begins to climb at a more manageable grade through beautiful forest on very narrow singletrack to a spectacular vista at mile 8 where you meet the Edge Loop road. Believe me, you'll know when you reach the view! A right turn on the road takes you to another neat vista looking down on your route.

Retrace the route back to the start. It is possible to go on around the Edge Loop this way but the opposite direction is much more desirable. (See 'Edge Loop' on page 36)

Hunters Canyon to the Edge

What is it: A long way to ride the Edge Loop via Hunters Canyon
Where do I start: End of pavement on 18 Road/Hunters parking/21 Road
How long: 34-mile loop with many variations
Climbing: 3400'
Who rides this: Super fit, likes super long, enjoys technical
Why's it cool: Very long with a very big climb
When to ride: April - October (avoid hunting season)

Hunters Canyon is a technical play spot, famous jeep trail and proposed wilderness with the biggest climb in our area. Atop this climb it joins the Edge Loop. Using the race course to begin and end this is BIG, technical, steep and a lot of singletrack. It's rarely done.

As 18 Road turns dirt, park and ride east on 2-track. Begin paralleling a fence; don't cross cattle guard (1.0). Continue along fence until forced through a gate; hang an immediate right on singletrack. This fast track heads due east to a road jct. at 3.5 miles. Our trail continues straight ahead staying left above the wash just ahead.

Singletrack splits at a steep hill; stay right, and continue out the trail to a KEY LEFT at obscure intersection at 5.0 miles (missing this still gets you to 21 Road). Heading north across grassland you meet a road at 6 mile. Turn right on this 2-track, then left heading towards the Bookcliffs. You'll meet a main road at 6.8 (21 Road); a right and a left puts you on Hunters Canyon Road (toward the huge canyon).

Continue out the road to a key left turn at 13 miles. Singletrack crosses a creek; turn left on the road and cross again at 14.5 miles.

Continue up this old road into the canyon; continue up the canyon bottom even when the road seems no more. It's very technical with many water crossings in a deep narrow canyon. High up, the road will reappear climbing out to the left — climb! Top out at a 4-way junction with the Edge Loop, 18 mile. Turn left on the Edge Loop (use Edge Loop directions). At the cow pond just below 18 Road parking, turn left (30 mile) for a finish via the race course singletrack (see Chet Peach Race Course), or descend the road. The start is 4.3 miles left down 18 Road.

NOTE: *For very strong riders only, and local knowledge is essential in route finding. Do not attempt without a map (Lat 40)! Hunters Canyon has huge flash flood risk, rain=NO GO! Options abound.*

DOUGLAS PASS RIDES

The Mirror

What is it: A huge ridge ride with awesome vistas
Where do I start: 15 miles north on 16 Road
How long: Out-and-back up to 30 miles
Climbing: 2,100 feet
Who rides this: Anyone can – it's long but very scenic, low tech
Why's it cool: Nice climb and an awesome ridge run at 7,500'
When to ride: May - September (overrun in hunting season)

This is an area with vast potential for exploration on gas roads. I will describe a great out-and-back ride, and you can always explore further. Be respectful of private property and never mess with gas wells or gates. This ride is a special place, don't let the word 'roads' scare you. It's true 2-track for much of the way and rarely driven or even visited outside of hunting season.

This ride begins on 16 Road as it enters the canyon of Big Salt Wash 15 miles north of Fruita. Of the many places to park, I like the junction right at 12.5 miles or the junction left at 14 miles by the tree. You can drive further to shorten the ride.

Begin riding up the dirt road along Salt Creek. Easy climbing and creek-side cottonwoods. Pass Garvey Canyon on the right, continue up the canyon passing a few spur roads on your left and a ranch on right. At 4.4 miles past Garvey, pass Post Canyon Road on your left* and at 4.9 turn left on Lapham Canyon road, marked by a short climb to a cattle guard and gate.

A long but pleasant grade climb leads to great views of the Bookcliffs and beyond. When you think you have reached the top make a sharp left at the gas well and climb a bit more to the true summit, a flat atop the ridge at 7,400', at junction by a fence.

Turn left along this fence and descend to a junction. *At the bottom of the hill, this is the top of Post Canyon, an optional steep descent; turn right and climb back to the ridge. At the next junction a left brings you to a viewpoint; to continue on, make a right through the fence and descend a rutted 2-track. From here the road runs the ridge for miles, ending in a meadow at the 16 mile point. Retrace your route from any turn-around point. The future may make this a loop to the start 1200 feet below. (Descending Post Canyon is VERY steep and for technical, advanced riders only)

59

Flight of Icarus

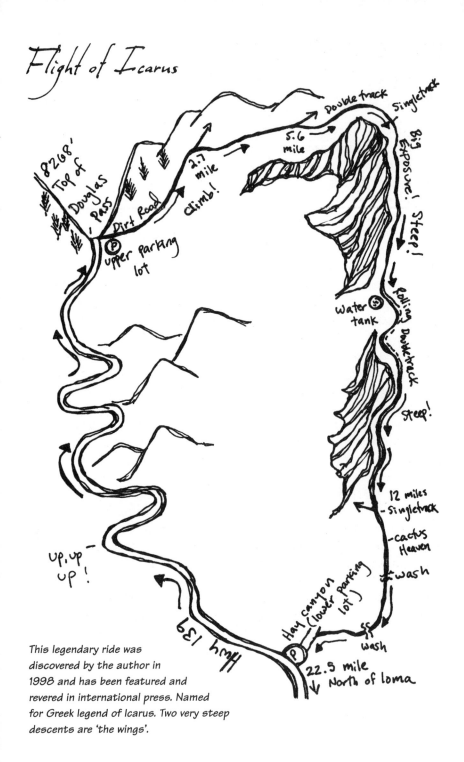

This legendary ride was discovered by the author in 1998 and has been featured and revered in international press. Named for Greek legend of Icarus. Two very steep descents are 'the wings'.

Flight of Icarus

This trail was posted closed in fall of 2003 due to Hunter concerns. The BLM and MTB advocates will work to resolve any issues on this legendary trail and it will eventually be re-opened; most likely with seasonal closure. Do NOT ride during hunting season.

What is it: Scenic road to spectacular trail at 8,000 feet
Where do I start: Douglas Pass / or mile mark 24
How long: 15 mile shuttle / 25 mile loop
Climbing: 1800'
Highlight: Spectacular ridgeline singletrack
Who rides this: Technical skills and altitude fitness required
Why's it cool: High country, cool and a legendary descent
When to ride: June till hunting season starts

The connection of trails used by hunters in the fall and an old BLM water project dozer cut yielded this incredible adventure ride. Trail runs an exposed ridgeline at 8,000 feet. Seriously for skilled riders only!

To shuttle, leave a car at Hay Canyon, 22.5 miles north of Loma (mm24), on Hwy 139. Shuttle to Douglas Pass at 33.5 miles. Park car at top of Douglas Pass. The ride begins climbing up gravel road to right (east) of the pass. Top this ridge (top-o-the world) at 1.5 mile. Continue on gravel road, through another saddle & climb, to a right turn at 'Y' intersection at 2.7 miles on dirt road.

Continue out ridgeline road with views well into Utah to a right turn on a seldom used Jeep/ATV trail at 5.6 miles, near the top of a climb. Two steep ups on this 2-track dead ends in a gravelly area on top of the ridge. Continue down a rutted track, heading toward the edge. At an ATV turn-around pick up a faint trail; if in doubt head towards the cliff – the trail trends left along the cliff.

The next section is indescribable, amazing exposure, huge descent on narrow 1-track. Please ride the line, keep this one narrow. At the bottom of the ridge join an old road, now singletrack, and continue out the ridge. Stay left, at 10.5 miles, drop off the left side of the ridge, around the dead tree and descend wildly down the second wing. Once in the canyon bottom, at 12.0, turn left on singletrack and stay left of the creek. At 14.4, before a fence, drop right across the creek cow path which leads to the road, gate and Hwy 139 at 15 miles.

Big exposure...great views.

Jason (Edge Cycle fabricator)
riding Flight of Icarus

Flight of Icarus photos by
Craven Daily and Chet Peach

See? It's not <u>that</u> steep!

Douglas Pass to the Mirror

One gigantic shuttle ride, or a 2-3 day tour.

What is it: A giant-killer at altitude
Where do I start: Douglas Pass with a car at mile marker 12
How long: 44.5-mile shuttle
Climbing: 4000' plus, and top at 8,800'
Who rides this: Only the very few, very fit, and very skilled
Why's it cool: Covers such a huge section of the Bookcliffs
When to ride: June - September (not good during hunting season)

This is a ride for the truly fit and true adventurers. You must carry a map, be prepared to spend the night and do not ride unprepared. This is big, wild country filled with dangers and seldom visited by people. You will not find any help on this loop; there is one bail-out point and only one. To shuttle, leave car in lot past mile post 11 on Hwy. 139. (10 mi N of Loma)

From Douglas Pass, ride east on the dirt road, stay right at 2.75 miles and continue out the ridge road. Pass all spurs and turn right at 9.6 mile, still on dirt road. Pass a gate at 10 mile and make a key right turn across from a gate at 11.5, on a very faint 2-track (do not go left as it is private property).

Descend this 'long point' to the end and drop steeply on very rocky old road. Near the bottom make the obvious left; then at 16.5 turn right on another jeep road. Continue descending with several water crossings. Stay right at 18.5 and as the valley opens up watch for a key left at 19.5 miles. (Option: continue down this valley to Hwy 139; at mm24 it crosses private land and should only be used in emergency.)

Turn left on ATV trail, cross the creek and begin climbing! This steep track climbs 1200' in just over a mile and traverses to the right. Stay left at the only junction and climb through a saddle and traverse to the main saddle at 26 miles.

At this open intersection marked with a fence and panoramic views, turn left (option right) and descend to a right at 27.2 and another right at 30, at Big Salt Wash. This major dirt road descends to the mouth of the canyon to a right turn at 36 (before the ditch passes under the road) on 'X' road. This dirt road will hug the front of the Bookcliffs and finally descend to Hwy 139 at 44 mile. Turn left on Hwy 139 to shuttle car at 44.5 miles.

First completed ride of this epic was 2001: Skip Hamilton, Jason Grove, Jeff Mohrman, Kevin Foote, Mike Curiak and Troy Rarick...what a crew, what a ride!

Over The Edge, Edge Cycles
and the Fruita Fat Tire Festival
join the Fruita Fat Tire Guide
in supporting our local advocacy groups

I·M·B·A
International Mountain
Bicycling Association

Join IMBA at **www.imba.com**

COLORADO PLATEAU MOUNTAIN BIKE TRAIL ASSOCIATION, INC

Join COPMOBA at **www.copmoba.com**

Author and the Fruita gang (Jon Rizzo, Kevin Foote, Jason Grove, Mark Roberts and Jerry Daniels) on Zippedy-Do-Da in the Bookcliffs. Rich Etchberger photo.

There was a storm brewing in the Bookcliffs.

Chutes & Ladders in the early days, summer 1995.

Photo by Rich Etchberger

Rabbit Valley

Now a part of the vast Colorado Canyons National Conservation Area or NCA. This area will be secured as another of Fruita's recreation centers. Rabbit Valley was established as a trail system by motorcycle riders and horseback riders. It had been adopted as an official trail system in the 80s and now is part of a much larger, better managed recreation area.

Rabbit Valley is the second section of the Kokopelli's Trail as it heads out of Colorado into Utah. But even more relevant are the miles of shared-use singletrack loops in and around the valley itself. The area is a bit more sandy than the other Fruita trails and the singletrack is motorized so it is not nearly the narrow stuff you'll find in other areas, but is still fairly entertaining and worth a visit. It is also a help to know that the most destructive users seem to stay closer to the parking lot and the trails get much better as you get farther out from I-70.

The Westwater Area west of Rabbit Valley proper holds miles of great riding. In the 90s several user-created trails appeared farther out from Rabbit Valley reaching into Utah. The Overlook Trail, Westwater Mesa and the Zion Curtain are among these 'newer' routes and are still fairly narrow, technical and very much worth seeking out for the skilled rider seeking a new experience.

Due to the sandy soils, this area is a general good bet in wet times. The soil is not all sand and pure 'snowmelt' will make it a muddy bentonite mess, but in light rain it is still quite ridable.

Access:

Main Rabbit Valley Parking. Exit I-70 at exit #2, 17 miles west of Fruita, turn left across overpass, and left again to 2nd parking lot. Plenty of parking and restrooms are available.

Westwater trailhead. Exit I-70 at the Westwater exit #225; 23 miles west of Fruita. Turn left (south) under interstate and park left in 0.1 miles in the large parking area near the gas wells with a 2-track road heading left (south). The Kokopelli's trail is 1.5 miles up the right fork of this road.

NOTE: most of this area is in the Colorado Canyons National Conservation Area which is being planned as this book goes to press. All these rides will remain open and in the future a few new ones may appear. Please respect any closures due to this area's protection.

Western Rim

OPTIONS: add the extra singletrack at
8.5 miles for an extra six miles. Or use
this as an option on the Kokopelli's
Trail. Or shuttle this ride to the
Westwater exit in Utah .

I-70

Trailhead #1

Trail #2

Kokopelli

Trail #2

Trailhead Alternative
(mcDonald creek)

Kokopelli

Kokopelli

N

singletrack

Colorado

(No Beer)
UTAH

(Beer)
colorado

Colorado River

The Western Rim

What is it: Long semi-loop with a variety of fun terrain
Where do I start: Rabbit Valley exit #2 or McDonald trailhead
How long: 15-mile loop from exit 2, 15 from McDonald Creek
Climbing: 1000'
Highlight: Slickrock & singletrack on canyon rims
Who rides this: Intermediate singletrack skills & fitness, long
Why's it cool: Singletrack & slickrock along the Colorado River
When to ride: Anytime without snow or snowmelt

A superb MTB experience! Singletrack mixed with slick rock. This could be the finest ride we have in the Rabbit Valley area. Certainly worth a trip if you enjoy fast, scenic, narrow singletrack with too many surprise airs to count.

The 20-mile option begins at Rabbit Valley parking area. Ride SW on trail #2 following singletrack and jeep road that rejoin the Kokopelli's at mile 2.1; follow this road west to the McDonald Creek trailhead at mile 2.6.

The 15-mile ride: drive the Kokopelli's from exit #2 to McDonald Creek at mile 2.6, saving 5 miles.

From McDonald Creek Trailhead (re-zero miles here) continue west across a wash and turn right onto trail #2. Cross a road at 1 mile, stay left at junction (right bypasses a cool steep hill). The #2 meets the Kokopelli's at 2.5 miles. Continue straight across road.

Cross the Kokopelli's road, descend a trail and join a road staying left. This sandy ATV track begins to descend; keep left until it really starts to drop, then turn right on singletrack at 3 miles, (by a tree) before halfway down. Once you've made this right out of the sand onto singletrack you're on the 'western rim.' This trail follows the rim and provides numerous thrills for the next five miles.

A fun descent at mile 8 brings you to a road at 8.5 miles; turn right on this road and climb to the Kokopelli's at 9.5 miles. (Crossing the road at mile 8.5 is more singletrack leading to the Westwater Mesa trail.)

Turn right on the Kokopelli's Trail and ride this cool old stagecoach road back to the trail #2 junction at mile 11.6 (same as mile 2.5). Turn left on the #2 and retrace your route via a 'rip roaring' descent back to the start at mile 14.4 or 19.6.

Kokopelli's Trail
AN EASY 2-TRACK DAY RIDE THROUGH RABBIT VALLEY

What is it: A ride that's scenic, fun and not real hard
Where do I start: Rabbit Valley exit #2, park in lot
How long: 5 to ... mile out-and-back on 2-track
Climbing: Minimal
Highlight: Rock towers, sunshine and bunnies
Who rides this: Minimal technical, mild fitness required.
Why's it cool: Winds through the rocks and cliffs of Rabbit Valley.
When to ride: Darn near 365 days a year, not even too bad wet

Fruita is known for its advanced riding and narrow singletrack. But sometimes there is call for a nice desert scenic cruise, and this is that ride. It's a great place to take novice riders, kids, families and riders working on their skills. It is a scenic jeep road ride but also has numerous options for exploring singletrack that paralleling the road. I will not get too fancy with mileage or directions. It is well-marked and easy to follow. As for distance, turn around when you have gone half as far as you want to. Options abound; the most prevalent is trail #2 that parallels this route.

From the parking area follow the road to the southwest; the road is well marked as the Kokopelli's Trail. This is your route out and back. A good destination is the McDonald Creek trailhead for a 5-mile ride and can be added in as a hike to Indian art (bring a lock for your bikes if you plan to hike much). There is a restroom here but no water so bring plenty. And if you hike, remember the return ride is a bit uphill.

For the more ambitious, you can ride all the way to the trail intersection and the Utah border. This out-and-back will give you a 10-mile ride and the option to return on the singletrack of trail #2 (to the right at the top of the climb on the Kokopelli's trail). Riding this far out will add a bit of climbing as well as a bit more challenge; returning via the #2 singletracks adds significant technical singletrack.

The Kokopelli's Trail continues 20 miles to the Westwater exit off I-70 and a possible shuttle ride between the exits. If you choose to do this follow the marked route well into Utah. The Kokopelli's makes a big climb at 18 miles. At the top turn right and then another right just ahead. You leave the Kokopelli's at this junction and follow a short jeep road NW directly to the I-70 Westwater exit.

Fruita Rotary Club,

Always ready to lend a hand!

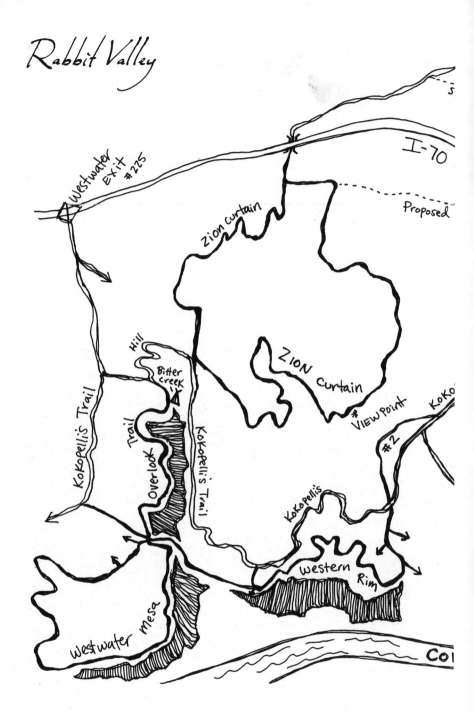

Rabbit Valley

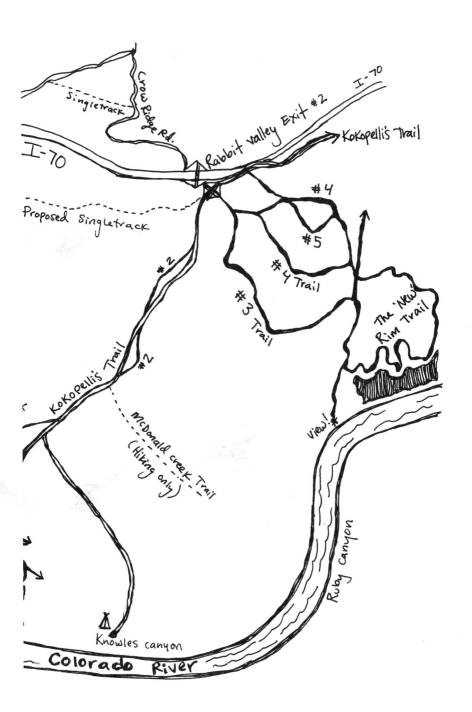

#3-#4 Loop

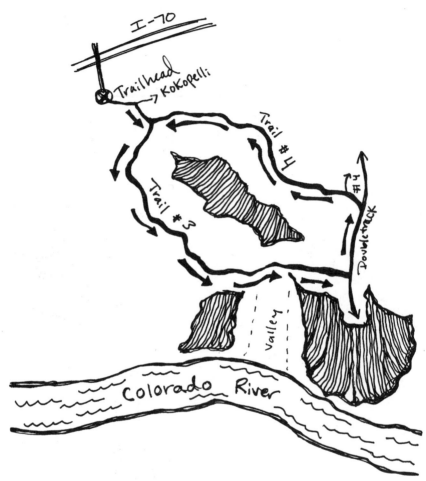

This Loop is one of my favorites for shop rides or any
other time you need a satisfying ride without burning
the entire day. Perfect for anyone who has a drive ahead,
it's right off the interstate and well worth doing. Two
significant climbs seem almost an unfair payment for
the amount of high quality descending you get to enjoy.

The #3-#4 Loop

What is it: Short fun Loop with some technical challenge
Where do I start: Rabbit Valley exit #2 Parking Lot
How long: 5 mile loop mostly singletrack
Climbing: 750'
Highlight: Cool moves among cool rocks
Who rides this: Mid to upper tech skills, medium fitness required
Why's it cool: Short, hard and fun. A great quick ride
When to ride: Anytime it's not muddy, often year round.

This ride crosses private land but everyone rides it and the BLM is making efforts to acquire that land.

Start from the parking lot just south of I-70 exit #2 (the second lot just left on the frontage road has a restroom). Begin riding back east on dirt frontage road, turning right just across cattle guard on a campsite road. Just after the campsite at the junction of 'trails' stay right, straight ahead, on the #3, paralleling the fence.

Rolling firm sand one-track leads you to a very steep hill and a portage for most everyone. I've never seen it ridden up. Above this hill the trail continues a rolling climb with some wonderful technical moves. A very technical traverse leads to a first technical then fast sandy 'roller coaster' descent down into the valley of the rim trail and a junction with a jeep road. (Rim Trail on next page)

Turn left on this jeep road, endure some sand to the base of a ledgy climb up the jeep road at 3 miles. At the top of this climb stay left, bypassing the first #4 junction and continue to the #4 trailhead that climbs through a small notch in the ridge. Again some technical descending and fast downhill leads you to a jumbled intersection; turn left (right will take you back to the #4 and #5). This trail passes through a track/play area and back to the start.

This trail is easily combined with the 'Rim Trail,' an option that will be described on the following page. It is also possible to turn right on the jeep road and go to a river view dead end if you need a little extra.

Even though this ride is technical in nature it is suitable for those seeking to expand their abilities. A less technical finish is found by following the #4 right at the top of the climb (3.2 miles), which will also return to the start.

The Rim Trail

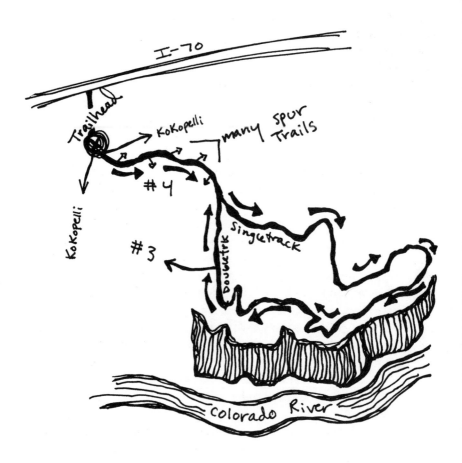

This trail is known to be sandy and is
intended to be very technically challenging.
It is on the map in the big parking lot.
It is pretty short, very pretty and used to
be narrow. River views and lots of sandstone make this a fun playful ride for the
technical rider yet accommodating for all.

The Rim Trail

What is it: Somewhat sandy technical singletrack
Where do I start: Rabbit Valley parking lot exit #2
How long: 4-mile all singletrack / 9 miles with #3-4
Climbing: 950'
Highlight: Ledges, rocks, and rock ledges
Who rides this: Fit rider seeking technical challenge & rocks
Why's it cool: Fun, scenic and filled with cool rock ledges
When to ride: Sandy soils hold up well year round, even in winter

From the parking lot there are several ways to get to this ride. The map shows starting on the #4 trail (just east of the cattle guard on the frontage road), descending the rocky jeep hill from 1.2 to the Rim trail left at its base. A suggested alternative is riding the #3 trail as described on the previous page, doing the 'Rim Trail' Loop, and finishing on the #4 trail as described in the previous ride.

From the lot: go east on the frontage road, right at the cattle guard, and follow #3 all the way to the dirt road at 2.8 miles. Turn left toward the big climb. At the bottom of this hill the 'Rim Trail' begins on your right. In summer if it's really dry and sandy we will often use the 2-track road you pass just before this trailhead; it joins the trail in one mile.

The first section is sandy ups and downs, usually climbable if you carry momentum or it's wet. In one mile you go from the base of the cliffs to overlooking the Colorado River in Ruby Canyon. Many ledges and challenges along the rim of the Colorado River canyon make this trail a play spot for the 'trials' aficionado. Beginner riders may hate it or find themselves walking a bit.

When the Rim Trail meets the jeep road, the same road as before, turn right, pass the #3 and head right back to the 'ledgy hill.' This time you climb the hill, and at the top you can turn right on the #4 trail for a fast trip home or stay left and finish the more technical half of the #4 loop, climbing over the ridge and getting some fast challenging descending. Stay left in the play area, and you're back to your start.

NOTE: It is possible to drive in closer to this ride on the road that leaves the Kokopelli's east of the lot just past the #5 trail. But why?

Overlook Trail

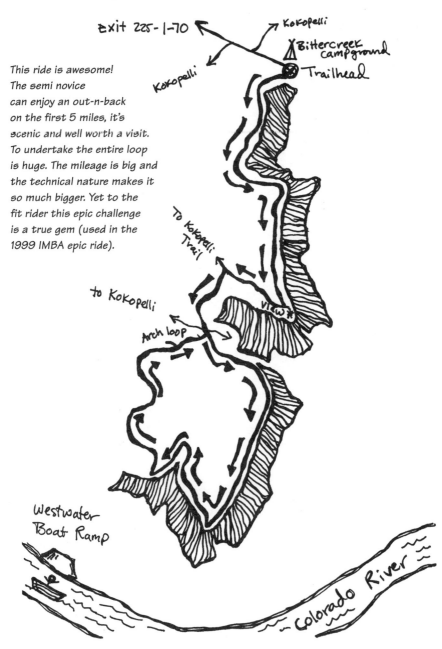

This ride is awesome!
The semi novice
can enjoy an out-n-back
on the first 5 miles, it's
scenic and well worth a visit.
To undertake the entire loop
is huge. The mileage is big and
the technical nature makes it
so much bigger. Yet to the
fit rider this epic challenge
is a true gem (used in the
1999 IMBA epic ride).

Exit 225 - I-70

Kokopelli

Kokopelli

Bittercreek campground

Trailhead

To Kokopelli Trail

to Kokopelli

view

Arch loop

Westwater Boat Ramp

Colorado River

Westwater Mesa / Overlook

What is it: A Gem! Sweet scenic singletrack with miles of options
Where do I start: Westwater exit #225 (just inside Utah)
How long: 23 miles with Westwater Loop; easily shortened
Climbing: 650' but feels like so much more
Highlight: Sitting on a cliff overlooking the river at half-way
Who rides this: Very strong technical rider seeking miles o' fun
Why's it cool: Mileage, all singletrack, really challenging & fun
When to ride: March - November

From Westwater exit, head south up the dirt road, stay right at .5 and then left at 1.1 and right again at 1.3 miles. A singletrack option goes left at 1.4; both lead to the campground at 2 miles.

From the campground, pick up the Overlook Trail right, behind the picnic table. Singletrack follows the rim affording awesome views and cool riding. Pass close to Kokopelli's at 2.6; stay left. Occasional 'bailout' trails go right but the main trail stays mostly near the rim. Meet a road in a jumbled area at 5.5 miles, turn right on this road (the trail across road is a hard option rejoining at 6.0).

Descend this road to a left on singletrack at 6.2 (all side trails are OK), a junction at 7.5, stay left. Overlook Trail meets a road at 7.6; climb to a left on Westwater Mesa trail at 7.7 (0.1 up road is Arch Junction), and bailout options (see Latitude 40 map).

Westwater starts with a vicious climb with some cool tech moves; this is just the beginning — the real challenges lie ahead. The next eight miles have no junctions and a plethora of really cool rock moves interspersed with wonderful river views. The trail climbs to a road at mile 15; follow this road left, using or ignoring several singletrack side routes, eventually descending to a road intersection at 15.6 miles (this is the same road just above previous mile 7.7).

From here turn right, follow the trail across the road (to previous mile 7.5) or drop to the Overlook trail (previous mile 7.6) and a return via your original route. At your previous mile 2.6 take the left onto the Kokopelli's road and another left back to your car at 23 miles.

OPTIONS: *from the intersection at 15.6 you may go left on the road to the Kokopelli's Road in 1 mile where a right follows the Kokopelli's back to previous mile 1.1 and a left drops to the paved Westwater road where a right leads back to the start.*

Zion Curtain

Built by the motorcycle trail riders, this loop
is new to MTB use and adds a nice big ride
to the Fruita arsenal. A big climb followed
by some really cool, occasionally hairy,
descents along a beautiful ridgeline,
finishing with some entertaining
singletrack and a 2-track cruise
for the final miles.

(Old US Hwy 50) M.80 Rd

Crow Ridge Rd.

Trailhead

to Rabbit Valley Exit

cross under

I-70

Future trail

Singletrack starts

dirt Rd.

Dirt Road

Pond

Dirt Rd.

'The Free World' (colorado)

The 'Not so Free world' (utah)

The Zion Curtain

What is it: Singletrack climb to high point above Rabbit Valley. Breathtaking views followed by breathtaking descent in a big loop
Where do I start: Rabbit Valley, go right and climb road to top*
How long: 20 mile loop
Climbing: 1600'
Who rides this: Fit with moderate tech skills (some gnarly bits)
Why's it cool: New, remote, scenic and a cool ridgeline up top
When to ride: March through November

The start of this ride may change under the Colorado Canyons NCA plan. For now we will cover the basic approach. If a new trail is built just remember you need to get to the I-70 underpass (in the wash bottom) between the Utah border and the Westwater exit, about mile marker 227.

Park at the top of the road. Climb north of the Rabbit Valley exit #2. Begin riding on this road (or west on the trail if still open), turning left on the first 2-track road. Descend this road for three miles to the I-70 underpass mentioned above. I will start mileage here.

Go under I-70 (south); climb the road to a singletrack left at 0.55 miles. Climbing and winding around cross a jeep road at 1.5, drop through a fun valley and cross the jeep road again at 2.5 miles. Meet and parallel a fence at 3 miles; this is the Colorado/Utah border, otherwise called 'the Zion Curtain'. At 4.3 miles a messy junction seems to work either way; I go left. Reach the rim and a grand view of Rabbit Valley and the Colorado river at 4.9 miles (for a 12-mile ride you could turn around here and retrace route).

Head right along the rim to a steep climb at 6 miles and the picturesque ridgeline at 6.2. This is the highlight section. Descend the trail crossing slickrock to a gnarly descent at 7.9 miles. Once down, un-pucker and roll the singletrack around the ridge; ignore the faint left at 9.5. Climb some cool rock moves and meet the Kokopelli's at 10.7 (Overlook trail is just one mile above us here); we turn right.

Ride the road north, staying left at the jeep road at 13.5, and passing our singletrack at 13.8, returning to the underpass at 14.3 miles. Return via original route back to the start.

OPTION: *from mile 10.7 a left on the Kokopelli's will return you to Rabbit Valley exit in 15 miles.*

Westwater Area / Rabbit Valley Extras

THE ARCH LOOP
What is it: Short cool loop or addition to Westwater Mesa
Where do I start: Where Westwater Road intersects Kokopelli's
How long: 7-mile loop / 3 mile addition
Who rides this: Seeking a short scenic loop or fun add-on
Why's it cool: There's a cool little natural bridge

Park where Kokopelli's meets the Westwater paved road 4 miles south of I-70 exit #225. Ride up the Kokopelli's 1 mile to a road right, and one more mile to the open 'arch junction' **(before dropping down); turn right on this smaller road, climbing a rocky hill (zero mileage). Bypass a trail right 0.1 after this turn; this is where you'll come out. Turn right on a trail at 0.6 and hard right again at 0.7, on a trail marked with orange tape. At a big rock drop into a wash at 0.25 you'll find the natural bridge at 0.35 miles

Continue around this short fun loop returning to 'arch junction' at 2.8; retrace your route to the start. Adding this to Westwater, the turn (0.7 here) is off the second spur after 15 miles.

OVERLOOK - WESTERN RIM CONNECTOR
What is it: Singletrack connection from Westwater to Western Rim
Where do I Start: where Overlook trail meets the road (** above)
How Long: 2.4 to Western Rim / 10 back to Westwater exit
Who rides this: Looking to create your own big loop?
Why's it cool: It opens up new loops and it's really fun!

From Arch Junction or mile 7.6 of the Overlook Trail, descend the steep road to a junction at the bottom in 0.5 miles; stay left. A very steep rocky climb at 1.0 places you on top of a sweet ridgeline section. Don't be fooled at 1.7 — turn hard left in the wash and reach the Western Rim and a road at 2.4 miles. From here, well, it's up to you. Left reaches the Kokopelli's at 4 miles where a right leads to Rabbit Valley; left leads to the Zion Curtain at 7.1 and a left there brings you back to Westwater exit in 9.2 miles.

As you can see, this little link opens up options to loop many of the other rides in this section. Or if you're ready, how about the Zion Curtain /Overlook — this connector and a finish on Western Rim / trail #2 back to Rabbit Valley exit at 34 miles? If that's not enough throw in Westwater Mesa to push it to 42...enjoy!

Grand Junction — Tabeguache Area

The Tabeguache area, or 'Lunch Loop' as it is also known, is a BLM/City Park located just to the west of downtown Grand Junction, Colorado. There really is no 'Lunch Loop' ride as such, but the name has stuck, probably from lunch hour rides for downtown workers. Now a maze of great singletrack offers miles of high quality riding for lunch hour and beyond. The name 'Tabeguache' is an Indian name that now resides on the 146-mile trail/route from Grand Junction south along the Uncompahgre Plateau. This is the trailhead and uses the jeep road as its route.

This area is the closest local riding to Grand Junction and is easily reached from town without driving. Some ride from Fruita using the riverfront trail as a connector. The trailhead described will be the Tabeguache trail parking area on Monument road.

To get here from Fruita: the I-70 overpass is CO 340. Follow it, all the way through the first light (Redlands Parkway)and continue almost to town; turn right at the second light (Monument Road). The parking area, with a trail sign, will be two miles ahead on your left.

If you're riding from Grand Junction: cross the Colorado River on Broadway, turn left on Monument Road, and turn left again on S. Redlands Road. In 0.3 miles wind up a hill and then continue straight ahead on Mira Monte to a trailhead on the curve ahead. This single-track, staying right, will lead you up to the eastern end of the Lunch Loop area, meeting the trail 'Kurt's Lane' above the parking lot.

Coming Soon...

A new challenging 'free ride' trail is being built from the top of Eagle's Wing down some sweet slickrock areas with some serious moves. This trail should be open in spring 2004. Thanks to Ryan Cranston and Chris Pipkin, BLM, for this vision and effort.

Holy Cross is being extended and re-opened. This book will describe it in its current state, knowing the end will be lengthened and re-routed throughout 2004 and finished by 2005. Thanks to Kevin Foote and COPMOBA for the efforts to re-open this trail.

The Riverfront Trail connector

The riverfront trail runs from Redlands Parkway (24 road), near Mesa Mall, to Monument Road in Grand Junction. It makes a nice easy stroll or a great connector to ride between Fruita and Grand Junction by connecting it with the river road. Parking is at either end and many other spots.

Ribbon — Andy's Trail

Almost 100% singletrack and much of that very challenging. This is a ride loved by the slow speed technical rider and appreciated for its wonderful scenery and close proximity to Grand Junction.

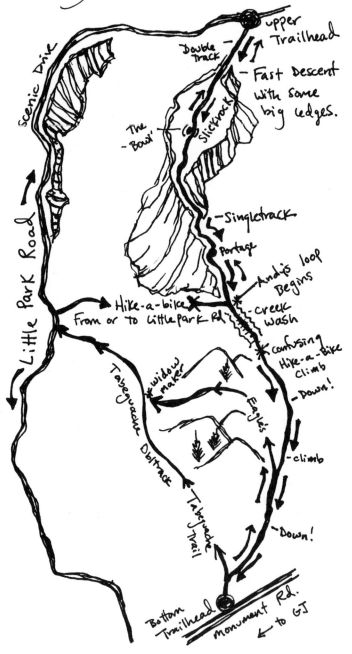

Upper Trailhead

Double Track

Fast Descent with some big ledges.

Scenic Drive

The 'Bowl'

Slickrack

Singletrack

Portage

Andy's loop Begins

Hike-a-bike From or to Littlepark Rd.

Creek Wash

Little Park Road

confusing Hike-a-bike Climb

Down!

Widow maker

Eagles

Tabeguache Dbltrack

climb

Down!

Tabeguache Trail

Bottom Trailhead

Monument Rd.

to GJ

Ribbon — Andy's Trail

What is it: A special blend of slickrock and singletrack
Where do I start: Tabeguache trailhead off Monument Road
How long: 7.5- to 13-mile loop
Climbing: 1200' short version; 2,200 long version
Highlight: Red rock paradise on your bike
Who rides this: They who love rock ledges and skinny trail
Why's it cool: It just is, I dare you to say it ain't...'A Ribbon of Rock!'
When to ride: March - November

From the parking lot head up the wash road; right at 0.5 on singletrack, switch backing up the Eagle's Tail — a wonder of little ledge 'ups' and cool tech moves. Remember it's proper to ride over these obstacles, not around. Riding around = bad form (+ very hard on the desert environment).

Climb in waves, passing Andy's Trail right at 1.0 and a left at 1.2 miles. Go left at a junction with Eagle's Wing at mile 2. Go right on the jeep road at the base of 'Widowmaker' hill. Climb this hill and run this jeep road all the way to the pavement at 3.3 miles; turn right. Descend this pavement watching for the second singletrack to the right (the one descending) at 3.7 miles. The Ribbon begins descending rapidly into the canyon below. Many steep pitches and cool moves drop you several hundred feet in 0.3 miles. to the wash below. A cool natural bridge/cave is worth checking out 2/3 of the way down. One last technical section lands you at a junction in the creek bottom at 4.1 miles.

For the short version, turn right on Andy's Trail. For the long (real) version turn left and climb the Ribbon to the top and back. The Ribbon climb requires careful trail attention and is in very fragile soils; stay on trail or rock. This adds six miles of really good riding.

Back at the wash bottom junction (previous mile 4.1), turn right on the creek bottom trail to a steep exit portage up and right out of the canyon. This climb involves some gnarly portaging and will eventually be re-routed. Once up top the trail begins a twisting turning descent that is well worth the trip. After this descent you'll have a perma-grin for the few short climbs back to the Eagle's Tail at 6.5 miles. (previous mile 1). Turn left and descend just over one mile to the start.

If you did the whole thing you'll be at 13.8 miles, or 7.7 miles if you opted for the short version. Many other options abound.

Eagle's Wing — Eagles Trail

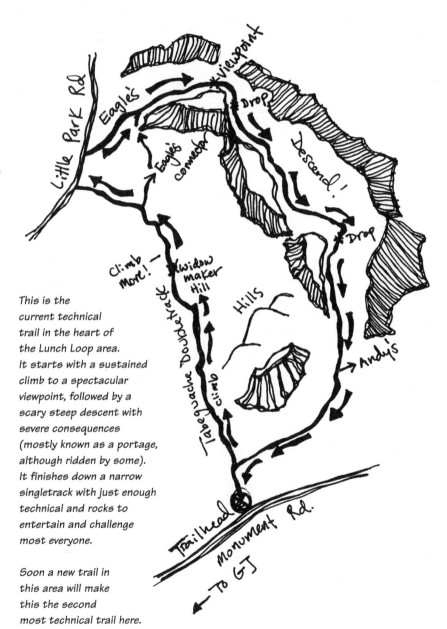

Little Park Rd

Eagle's

viewpoint

Drop

Descend!

Eagle's connector

Drop

Climb More! — Widow maker Hill

Tabeguache Doubletrack

climb

Hills

Andy's

Trailhead

Monument Rd.

To GJ

This is the current technical trail in the heart of the Lunch Loop area. It starts with a sustained climb to a spectacular viewpoint, followed by a scary steep descent with severe consequences (mostly known as a portage, although ridden by some). It finishes down a narrow singletrack with just enough technical and rocks to entertain and challenge most everyone.

Soon a new trail in this area will make this the second most technical trail here.

Eagles Wing — Eagles Trail

What is it: Short and very technical Loop
Where do I start: Tabeguache Trailhead on Monument Road
How long: 5-mile loop
Climbing: 900'
Highlight: 'One billion' rock moves
Who rides this: Skilled tech rider seeking climb, speeds & thrills
Why's it cool: Sweet moves in a spectacular setting
When to ride: March - November

The basic 'Lunch Loop' version begins by climbing up the jeep road across the wash from the parking area. Turn right on the road that climbs steep and right out of the wash at 0.5 miles. This road takes you up to the super-steep Widowmaker hill at 1.4 miles.

OPTIONAL START: *A new trail built in 2001/2002 climbs left from the parking lot up 'Kurt's Lane.' Climbing this and choosing uphill at all options you will reach the base of the Widowmaker at mile 1.8.*

Continue up the jeep road to a singletrack to the right just 1/4 mile above the Widowmaker. Turn right on this singletrack and climb to the ridge top and the 'Eagle's Wing' viewpoint at 2.2 miles (if you find yourself at the pavement, hang a right, and the next right back onto singletrack; this also climbs to the top at 2.2 miles).

I am uncertain who named this trail but I think it is one of the best-named. The view from this high point leaves no doubt what inspired it. For a short loop there is no finer destination than the summit of the Wing. From the ridge top a singletrack runs along the ridge to a higher point, crosses a small flat (the new trail opening 2004 will leave from this area), and then takes a very technical line down the spine of the ridge. The moves are big and the exposure huge! Safely at the bottom, watch for a trail left in 200 yards at 2.9 miles; turn left onto the 'Eagles Tail' (a right here returns you to the base of the Widowmaker). A left continues descending the ridge on a playfully rock-strewn technical trail. Pass the right at 3.7 and pass Andy's turnoff to the left at 3.9; continue descending the Eagle's Tail to the wash, where a left returns you to the start at 5 miles.

"The Ribbon"
Grand Junction -
Tabeguache Area

Thanks to Pete Fagerlin
for his photo contributions
and his support of Fruita
mountain biking.

www.petefagerlin.com

90

Clockwise from left: the author on "The Ribbon;" secret singletrack in Vernal, Utah; "don't bust the crust"... crypto soil on "The Ribbon." Photos by Pete Fagerlin and Rich Etchberger.

Tabeguache / Grand Junction

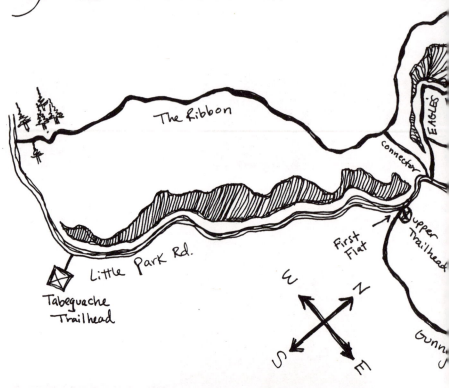

The Ribbon

EAGLES'

Connector

First Flat

Upper Trailhead

Little Park Rd.

Tabeguache Trailhead

W N S E

Gunn

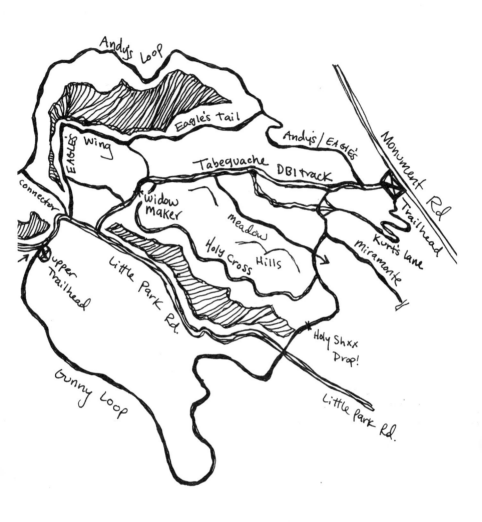

Andys Loop

Eagles Tail

EAGLES Wing

Andy's/EAGLES'

Monument Rd

Tabeguache DBI track

Trailhead

Connector

widow maker

Meadow Hills

Kurtis Lane

Holy Cross

Miramante

upper Trailhead

Little Park Rd.

Holy Shxx Drop!

Gunny Loop

Little Park Rd.

93

The 'New' Holy Cross

What is it: Creative rocky singletrack with endless surprises
Where do I start: Tabeguache Trailhead on Monument Road
How long: 6.5-mile loop
Climbing: 850'
Highlight: More fun than Moore Fun?
Who rides this: Challenge me baby, make me work for it
Why's it cool: From the creators of Moore Fun, more fun!
When to ride: March - November (or when frozen solid)

It's rare that a trail re-route becomes a good thing. Often it means making a trail easier and wider. Well, not here. Thanks to Kevin Foote and dozens of COPMOBA volunteers, this re-creation of a great trail is making it longer, harder and better than before. The theme here is technical rock moves laid out in creative ridable ways, very much in the style of Moore Fun in the Kokopelli's Loops.

From the parking lot, head left to the singletrack, switch-backing the hill east of the trailhead lot. This 'Kurt's Lane' trail climbs up the ridge to an old jeep road. Follow this road, passing one right that drops off the hill; continue arcing right up the ridge choosing uphill at all options until you reach the 'Lunch Loop' road and the base of the Widowmaker hill. Before you reach this hill the Holy Cross singletrack heads left across the meadow at 1.6 miles.

Once on Holy Cross there are no junctions or options – it is a continuous gem of a trail that will keep you very much on your toes, either by testing your bike-handling skills or because you're walking. Several very creative rock lines and a few option moves make this feel almost trials-like but with a tremendous flow. It's a very good trail and a project worth applauding. The final section which will extend this trail will not be christened until 2005.

But it will still go to the same place. Once the trail drops you out in a valley at an old road at 4.9 (new version will add .6 miles), go left on the road, becoming singletrack, and climb to a small rocky saddle at 5.2 miles. Here a left or a straight ahead will return you to your route and 'Kurt's Lane;' a right descends to the start at 6.5 miles (a right here will drop you back to town via Mirimonte Canyon to Monument Road).

94

OPTIONS FOR HOLY CROSS: *This ride is easily combined with others in this area. One suggestion; do the Eagle's Wing ride as described, but stay right at 2.9 miles, returning to the base of the Widowmaker and the start of Holy Cross. Once back at 'Kurt's Lane' you can descend or go left and complete a big figure-8 descending Eagle's Tail.*

Gunny Loop

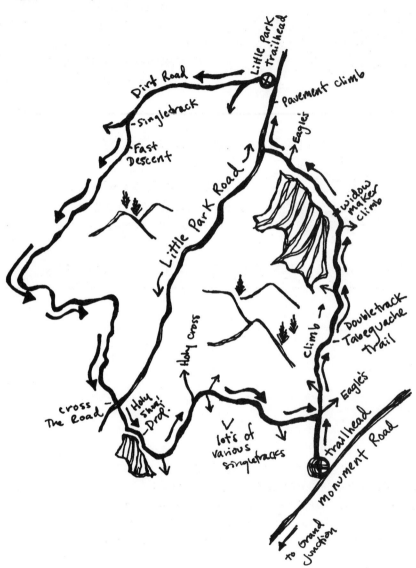

Little Park trailhead

Dirt Road

Singletrack

Fast Descent

Pavement climb

Eagle's

Little Park Road

widow maker climb

Doubletrack – Tabeguache Trail

Climb

Holy Cross

cross The Road

Holy Shit! Drop

lot's of various singletracks

Eagle's

trailhead

monument Road

to Grand Junction

96

Gunny Loop

What is it: A fast fun loop that combines well with others
Where do I start: Tabeguache Trailhead
How long: 8-mile loop
Climbing: 1250'
Who rides this: It's a bit rocky but with patience it can work.
Why's it cool: It can add a few good miles to any area ride
When to ride: Mid March - Mid November

The Gunny Loop as described can be done as a ride in itself, but is also done as a combination with other rides in the area. Almost every other ride described in this section can be used as a base for the Gunny Loop. I will pick up the ride from Little Park Road, which can be reached just above the Widowmaker hill on the Tabeguache Trail or just below the Eagle's Wing. It is also possible to drive to 'First Flats' parking area on Little Park Road just uphill from the Tabeguache/Ribbon trails.

Climb Little Park Road on pavement, passing the Ribbon on the right. Continue up pavement to a big parking area on the left. This is the 'First Flats' area (start mileage here). Turn left into this area on gravel road. In half a mile, not before, turn left again on gravel road to the Gunny Loop sign on a very rocky road at 0.75 miles. Singletrack begins descending to the left at 1.4 miles.

Now descend the very fast and rocky Gunny Loop trail, heading straight for the Gunnison River below. The trail will not reach the river but rather will curve left into a small valley and a challenging climb out the other side. The trail will descend again over some cool rock ledges to Little Park Road at 4 miles.

The singletrack resumes across the road and descends steeply into a valley and a 2-track at 4.6 miles. Turn left on the 2-track, stay right at Holy Cross exit, and follow singletrack right – climbing to a junction atop a rocky saddle at 5 miles.

If you parked at First Flat go left here; choose uphill at all intersections, back to the Widowmaker and climb to your car.

If you parked at the Tabeguache trailhead continue straight ahead, crossing the head of the small valley and a short climb out the other side. Descend to the trailhead.

If you rode from town turn right, then right again and descend Mirimonte Canyon to Monument Road.

OPTION FOR ROUGH CANYON TO WHITEWATER: *if you are riding as a loop head left after crossing the river and ride the streets north through town looking to pick up the 'Old Spanish Trail' which will return you to Grand Junction on dirt trail and 2-track. Once into town continue north across highway which will bend left, pick up the bike path behind the Middle School and ride it back into town along the river. Looping from Monument Road is a 44 mile Loop.*

Tabeguache Trail / Rough Canyon to Whitewater

What is it: Long ride on the Tabeguache Trail to Whitewater
Where do I start: Bangs Canyon Staging area on Little Park Road
How long: 25-mile one way / huge loop / jeep road
Climbing: 2,200'
Who rides this: Fit rider seeking not too technical ride
Why's it cool: Long, high and very remote...beautiful...long
When to ride: May - September

Unless you want the 40-mile version, this ride is a shuttle. Park a car in Whitewater, just south of Grand Junction on US 50 towards Montrose. There is parking near the river bridge on 141.

This long ride on a jeep road is actually good. It draws its quality from its length, remote setting and variety of riding. You begin on slickrock, do a huge climb on smooth dirt surface, cruise in high forest for miles, and then descend on a rock-strewn speedway back to the banks of the Gunnison River in Whitewater.

Park at the Bangs Canyon staging area on Little Park Road. The Tabeguache Trail is well marked and is the main route leaving the parking lot. It immediately begins descending a large slickrock bench and will continue the descent all the way to creek bottom. There is a cool waterfall in the spring just before the bottom; a good short ride.

Cross the creek and begin to climb. This long climb is rewarded by a roadside spring at 5.7 miles, marking the top of the climb. Now a joy of a forest cruise: the 2-track rolls through high piñon forest in a high cliff- banded valley.

Rolling more ups than downs tops you out in a higher, denser forest at the high point of the ride just after crossing Rough Canyon, which drops to the east. A junction here marks the high point, and a left begins the long, well-deserved descent into the desert valley below.

Near the bottom, at 21 miles, a trail (marked Tabeguache) heads right and descends to Highway 141. A left on this pavement brings you to the Gunnison River in just over a mile and the town of Whitewater just beyond.

Stagecoach / Palisade

What is it: Singletrack on an old stage road high above I-70
Where do I start: Palisade I-70 exit #42 / Palisade Brewery
How long: Out-n-back or 8-11 mile loop
Climbing: 1,800'
Who rides this: Those looking for a cool new ride in a very scenic place
Why's it cool: Riding the rim of the Bookcliffs above the valley
When to ride: Late February to first big snow (Nov/Dec)

This ride will be getting better access and marking as the City of Palisade undertakes support of this scenic historic trail. Its use has been limited by difficult access. Current access is to park off I-70 just east of the Palisade exit. (Go past, turn around at Cameo exit and park on the right, just past the I-70 river bridge). Check at the Palisade Brewery for newer information (and good beer) on future access and better marking of MTB rides.

From this trailhead climb the old stagecoach road, now singletrack, to the top of the Bookcliffs (0.4) along the rim, west to a junction of a trail left/road right at 1.8 miles. From here slickrock exploring lies ahead, a gnarly descent down the Bookcliffs is left, and a longer loop via jeep road descends right. I suggest retracing your route after some scenic exploration along the rim. This scenic ride will only get even better with new information and new trail coming soon.

After the ride, head back to Palisade Brewery for a good beer.

Grand Junction North

THE DESERT

This is desert riding north of GJ near the airport and running all the way to the 'Bookcliffs' trail system in Fruita. I have taken this out as a ride but it is worth mentioning in a general sense. Countless trails make it very difficult to describe a certain ride but miles and miles of opportunity abound. Here's the basic scoop...

Miles of trails, 2-track roads and dirt service roads make up a maze that is impossible to describe but fun to explore. Eventually some delineation and actual 'trails' may be designed and marked, but for the time being it is best to go with a mind to explore (or grab a local to guide you). It is very possible to ride from Fruita's trails to Grand Junction along these routes, even largely on singletrack.

Access to this GJ section is best via two options:

North on 29 Road from Patterson (F Road): park just after the canal before crossing I-70. Ride the dirt road west till you can duck under I-70 via a concrete access tunnel. From here do not cross fences into airport property. Explore north and west – east leads to heavy motorcycle and ATV activity area.

From Horizon Drive exit off I-70: head toward the airport, turn left on G Road just before entering the airport. In just over a mile turn right on 27¼ Road and park just past the pavement end and explore singletracks right (a ride called 'roller coaster') and left, which can lead you all the way to Fruita.

High Country Rides

Late summer brings hot temps to the valleys, but fear not. Fruita is surrounded by Colorado high country. We have included a few rides from our upcoming 'High Country Guide to Western Colorado,' one from each of our most nearby high altitude areas.

Turkey Flats - Pinion Mesa, above the National Monument
The Grand Mesa, high mesa east of town reaching 10,000 feet
Uncompahgre Plateau, south of town with miles of trails
Douglas Pass, high country north of Fruita, home of the Flight of Icarus

All of these areas are within an hour of town, reach elevations of 7-10,000 feet and summer temps in the 60-70 degree range. The rides shown here are just a sample and are some of the best.

Rich Etchberger

Turkey Flats... some of the sweet singletrack high above Fruita.

Turkey Flats — Piñon Mesa

What is it: Summer high country singletrack treasure
Where do I start: Fruita Reservoir #2 picnic area
How long: 10 miles as a figure-8 loop (80% singletrack)
Climbing: 1,200 feet climbing at over 8,000 feet high
Who rides this: Hot rider seeking cool summer singletrack
Why's it cool: Yeah it's cool, but the riding is really awesome too
When to ride: June - September

This bastion of mountain paradise less than an hour from Fruita/Grand Junction holds a combined loop of spectacular forest and lakeside singletrack. Sitting on Piñon Mesa, water reservoirs and fishing lakes, deer, elk, bear, and wild turkey provide a lush setting.

Drive through Colorado National Monument to Glade Park (ask directions at gate). From Glade Park 4-way, at a small store (zero miles), head south on 16.50 Road past 'Mud Springs Campground' (6.8 miles). Stay right at the fork (8 miles). Avoid all spurs. Park at the picnic ground (10 miles); left at the road to Reservoir #1.

Begin the ride back out to and continuing up the main road. In one mile turn left onto the 'Turkey Flats' singletrack. Climb nicely in lush grass to a 'flat' and an intersection at 2.25 miles. Turn left here (we will return via the right), exiting the lower end of the meadow. This stretch passes ponds, elk and brings you to the Res. #1 road at 3.5 miles; turn right. Climb the road to trailhead parking lot at 4.5 miles; continue up along the lake shore. At the upper end of the lake the trail begins to climb, steeply in sections, through aspen forest to an ATV trail at the top (6.5 miles); turn right/west.

The one key turn is the right off this ATV trail onto singletrack at 7.5 miles. If you reach the viewpoint/road descent, turn back 1/4 mile. Singletrack heads north into the forest. Follow this trail as it begins a wonderful descent back to the 'Flats' and the junction we have been to before; now at 9 miles.

Turn right again and do the really cool section across to the Res. #1 road again...I know you don't mind (obviously you can bail left here also to the start at 11 miles). When you reach the Res. #1 road again at 10.25 miles turn left this time and descend to your car/picnic area at 12 miles. Hopefully you brought the cooler and some weenies for this perfect picnic post-ride setting.

Grand Mesa — Wild Rose/Kannah Creek

What is it: A high country adventure challenge; seriously
Where do I start: Wild Rose trailhead on Lands End road
How long: 20-mile shuttle optional out-n-back 10.4 miles
Climbing: 800' 10,000 feet high
Highlight: Descending Kannah Creek Trail / not being lost
Who rides this: Strong rider, map skills, advanced tech skills
Why's it cool: A big ride that is rarely done but should be
When to ride: June - September (avoid in hunting season)

This ride is big, awesome and very hard. It is rewarding and scenic with miles of killer good trail. It is also hard to follow at times, easy to get lost and will make you carry your bike over a hundred downed trees in a bad year. I will not try to describe it mile by mile, you need a detailed map and the ability to read it. Leave a car at the turnoff or at Kannah Creek trailhead 7miles up Road GS.00.

From Wild Rose PG off Lands End Road ride south on FS 702, a wild rose/coal creek trail. Pass descending Coal Creek FS703 at 5.2miles (this will reach Kannah Creek in 5miles) just after Deep Creek Trail joins from above. The key turn is at 10 miles where a jumble of livestock trails confuses the descending trail FS727; descend this jumbled trail (continuing on reaches Carson Lake /Kannah Creek trail in 2.8 miles). Once you find 'the trail' you will dump out in a grassy meadow, losing it again. Look to the lower left corner of the meadow for the trail (not the game trail traversing to the second meadow). It reaches Kannah Creek trail after crossing the creek itself at 12 miles; turn right and follow this FS706 to Kannah Creek trailhead at 19.4 miles.

Uncompahgre — Little Creek/ Corral Fork Loop

What is it: One of many Uncompahgre singletrack gems
Where do I start: Past Big Creek reservoir; 14miles west of Whitewater on C141, 9.5 south on Divide Rd, right 4.5 to Big Creek trailhead at 6.0
How long: 10-mile loop, 90% singletrack
Climbing: 900'
Highlight: Narrow singletrack almost overgrown with grass
Who rides this: Decent rider craving summer singletrack rewards
Why's it cool: Meadow & forest singletrack gets no better than this
When to ride: June (late) to hunting season

There is so much up here – camp and explore. This will get you started and the upcoming *High Country Guide* will have much more. Riding up here is perfect mountain fun. Not overly technical but always a bit here and there. Great views, wildlife and running streams. Over the Edge does an annul campout here if you need a group intro; check on www.otesports.com for info.

Park by the creek as directed above. Ride up the 'Corral Fork' trail on the right side of the creek, staying right at 1.0 miles (you'll return via the left trail). Gradually climbing in a huge meadow you may see deer, turkey or even black bear. It gets a bit steeper at mile 4 and you reach the top, the 'Rim Trail' road, at 5 miles.

Turn left on the rim trail road (right goes to an overlook, and hard right descends back to your car). Climb over a rise and turn left on a 2-track just before a gate at 5.6 miles. Descend this 'Cabin' jeep trail for just over half a mile and watch for a trail post in the meadow to the left. This is 'Little Creek' trail – catch it, descend and enjoy. You'll want more when you see the start at 10 miles.

The Mirror

Fruita versus Moab

WHY MOAB IS BETTER THAN FRUITA:

Deep sand imitates high mileage.
Where else can you get two great singletracks right next to each other.
Double Wide so you can share a bong with your buddy.
Jeeps carry beer.
If you count the highway...every ride is a loop.
Fill your Camelback™ with Utah beer and still stay hydrated.
'Connect the Dots' is way fun for the kids.
Chile Pepper Bike Shop...'Chile Fest'!
Where else can you get 'sponsored' to drink?
Sand is sexy.

WHY FRUITA IS BETTER THAN MOAB:

Mexican food & pizza, the basic food groups.
Real beer is served in wranglers.
Over the Edge Sports...'Sausage Fest'!
We have 'Tater' ....buddy....
Mike the Headless Chicken Day.
Crossing Aspen Street, the new extreme sport.
Fewer annoying red rocks.
Surprise trail closures keep you coming back.
Tractors and mullets.
Sex is legal!

(Made up by Anne & Troy, no harm intended)
All in fun, we really appreciate our brothers behind the Zion Curtain. With Moab just over an hour away it's a perfect destination when Fruita has a muddy day, and a must-do combo trip for anyone who has never been before.

Fruita singletrack is a wonderful thing, but who can dispute the beauty of Moab's red rock desert? It's fitting that Kokopelli's Trail connects two of the greatest mountain bike towns in the west. What a great place to be!

The Chet Peach Story

We were all standing at the bottom of the Horsethief Bench drop-in and here comes a rider making it all, clean and apparently easily. As this rider pulls up to us we see it's Chet Peach and he is riding a fully rigid singlespeed with 2.1 tires. Chet has been here since the beginning. He was the behind-the-scenes guy who walked for miles through the pinion juniper desert to find the routes that became the classic trails of Fruita. He has an uncanny ability to spot a line that, once built, becomes a legendary section of trail. It is his influence that made the trails in the Bookcliffs the best example of flow. It's Chet's hand too in some of the most legendary moves on Moore Fun.

In spite of his involvement in Fruita he is far from a local hero — even sometimes 'dis-liked' or found a bit offensive. Chet's life is like his trails: unique, original and true to the heart. He kind of marches to his own drummer, but it's endearing if you give him a chance. He's the kind of guy you wish would keep it down in the bar; he's the one who thinks it's fun to ride out well after dark and finds it inspiring be hopelessly lost, especially if he has victims along. It seems every time you ride with Chet it's to check out some new trail, or a new place, or to try this move no one has ridden yet over and over again.

We want to make sure Chet Peach's legend in Fruita mountain biking lives on. He brought together great people, showed us all new ways to look at things (even if they were wrong), and kindled a fire in all who want this to be the best MTB town on the planet. Daring to be different and dreaming to be above the rest are qualities that define how Fruita came to be.

Chet is still around, but no one ever seems to know when he will turn up. He's a bit elusive — almost "imagined" it seems. And as you ride Fruita's classic singletrack lines remember the passion and the people that went into making it so. But that's coming from me. I know Chet would say, "Ah hell, just enjoy it," and not care for a minute that you knew who he was or how it came to be. But we know, we remember and we appreciate. Chet has given a gift to us all: the gift of Fruita mountain biking and the chance to be a part of a place that stands as a monument to the true individual.

Thanks, Chet, for everything.

IMBA's Kevin and Pete winning the Clunker Crit in the Fruita Fat Tire Festival 2001

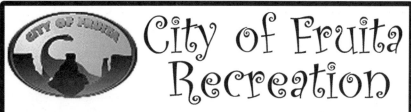

City of Fruita Recreation

"Come out and play!"

Other Events in Fruita:
May - Mike The Headless Chicken Festival
May - Fruita Triathalon
June - Dinosaur Days
June thru August - Thursday Variety Show @ Civic Center
7:30 pm

City of Fruita Recreation Department
325 E. Aspen, Fruita CO 81521

Office: 970-858-0360 Fax: 970-858-0210 Web: wreck@fruita.org

Local events

Annual Fruita area events:

Fruita Fat Tire Festival
The last Friday in April marks the weekend
April 28 - May 1, 2005
Good times with great people; rides, events, expo and beer
2005 10th year anniversary celebration and a new 24 hour event the weekend before the festival.

Mike the Headless Chicken Days
The second weekend in May
Food and fun surround the tale of Mike the headless Chicken

Tour of the Valley
The last Saturday in August
Road ride around the valley, 40-60 and 100 miles

Fruita Fall Festival
The last weekend in September
Live music, food vendors, beer garden in the streets of Fruita

24 Hours of Moab
Early October every year
It is what it is

Chet Peach BBQ
The third Saturday in October
BBQ, beer, urban ride and a celebration of the fall season

Moab Fat Tire Festival
The last weekend in October
Another good excuse to come ride

For more info- www.fruita.org
Fruita Event Calendar at www.otesports.com

The White Pages

For all your needs while riding here.
(Western Colorado Area Code is: 970)

ANTIQUES
Sweet Pea Antiques
Unique selection of antiques and collectibles
220 E. Aspen, Fruita 858-4301

ATTORNEYS
Barcott Law Office
Joseph Barcott
127 N. Cherry, Fruita 858-8230

BANKS
Community First
141 N. Park Square, Fruita 858-3682

BED & BREAKFASTS
Stonehaven B&B (see ad inside front cover)
Beautiful historic home, bike friendly
798 N. Mesa, Fruita 858-0898

BICYCLE SHOPS --
Chile Pepper Bike Shop (see ad on page 95)
Our 'home away from home' shop
550 1⁄2 North Main, Moab 435-259-4688

**Over The Edge Sports
(see ad on page 24)**
Where it all started
202 E. Aspen, Fruita 858-7220

Poison Spider Bicycles
Great high end Moab shop
497 N. Main, Moab. 800-635-1792

BICYCLE TOURS --
Rim Tours (see ad on page 95)
Day tours and multi day tours
1233 S. Hwy 191, Moab. 800-626-7335

Western Spirit
Multi day tours to a huge variety of locations
Mill Creek Dr., Moab   www.westernspirit.com
800-845-2453 <http://www.westernspirit.com. 800-845-2453

BREWERIES
Palisade Brewery (see ad page 100)
The brewery we all love and frequent
200 Peach Ave, Palisade 464-7257

COFFEE HOUSES
Colorado Java House
Hot chicks, cold drinks
502 Colorado Ave. Grand Junction 255-1100

CHIROPRACTORS
Mt. Garfield Chiropractic
Jerry Speight, D.C.
316 E. Hwy 6&50, Fruita 858-8682

GASOLINE & CONVENIENCE STORES
Conoco/Go Fer Foods (see ad page 12)
Circle Park, Fruita
Loma Country Store, Loma

Monument Shell & Mini Mart
Next to Wendy's at the Fruita exit off I-70

HOTELS

Balanced Rock Motel
126 S. Coulson, Fruita 858-7333

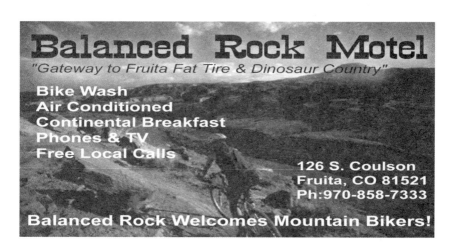

Comfort Inn
Hot tub, pool, bike friendly
400 Jurassic Ave, Fruita. 858-1333

Holiday Inn
Close to the airport off of Horizon Drive, indoor pool
755 Horizon Dr. Grand Junction 888-489-9796

Super 8
Across the freeway....handy to all
399 Jurassic Ave, Fruita. 858-0808

West Gate Inn
Just five minutes from Fruita; first sponsor of Fruita Fat Tire Festival!
2210 US Hwy 6&50, Grand Junction 800-453-9253

La Quinta Fruita....
Opening soon!

INVESTMENT BROKERS --
Waddell and Reed
Thomas McNamara
127 N. Cherry, Fruita 858-0730

MASSAGE THERAPIST --
Professional Bodyworks
When you're done with your ride, go get a massage!
316 E. Hwy 6 & 50 261-8101

NIGHTCLUBS
Boomers Jazz and Blues Club
Great atmosphere in downtown GJ, also serves some good grub
436 Main, Grand Junction 248-9022

PET BOARDING
Orchard Mesa Veterinary Hospital
Need a place to board your dog? Need veterinary assistance?
This is the place
2668 US Hwy 50, Orchard Mesa 241-9866

REALTORS
Fruita Realty
Our entire staff has bought houses from these ladies, simply the best!
303 W. Aspen, Fruita 858-9577

RESTAURANTS
Fiesta Guadalajara
Our favorite local Mexican restaurant, awesome margaritas!
103 Hwy 6&50, Fruita 858-1228

(970) 947-1670
503 Pine St.
Glenwood Springs, CO

(970) 249-2460
147 S. Main St.
Montrose, CO

Fiesta Guadalajara
A FAMILY MEXICAN RESTAURANT

OPEN 11:00 a.m. to 10:00 p.m. • 11:00 p.m. Weekends
(970) 255-6609
710 North Avenue
Grand Junction, CO

(970) 858-1228
103 Hwy. 6 & 50
Fruita, CO

Il Bistro Italiano
Amazing Italian food in a classy setting, 4 star!
400 Main, Grand Junction 243-8622

La Paninoteca
Grilled Panini sandwiches, salads and handmade Italian deserts
2211 N. 7th, Grand Junction 257-7000

Nepal Restaurant
Excellent Indian and Nepalese food
257 N. 5th St. Grand Junction 242-2233

Pablo's Pizza (see ad on page 122)
Huge selection of unique toppings, GJ's only gourmet pizza place
319 Main St. Grand Junction 255-8879

Suehiro Japanese Restaurant
Fresh Sushi in a fun atmosphere, one of our favorites!
541 Main St. Grand Junction.........................245-9548

VETERINARY CLINICS --
(see listing in Pet Boarding above)

We know you're going to want to support all these cool folks who support us!
Or, as Troy says (every chance he gets)...."support those who support the sport!"

Ride Ratings by Coolness and Difficulty

COOLNESS FACTOR
Coolness Factor is based on the ride quality, i.e. the 'Flow,' the 'Experience,' or possibly can be called the 'Laugh out Loud' and 'Whee Hee' factor. These are the rides that we, as locals who ride these trails all the time, covet as our favorites for all out fun.
Ratings: ☺ **'nice to meet ya' to** ☺☺☺☺☺ **'I think I'm in love'**

DIFFICULTY RATINGS
Difficulty Ratings are based on the technicality of the trail, rocks, ledges, and difficult moves. These are the trails that challenge our riding ability and offer the opportunity to improve our riding skills.
Ratings: ♦ **'nuttin to it' to** ♦♦♦♦♦ **'people ride this'?**

FITNESS FACTOR
Fitness Ratings are based on how hard your heart will beat on this ride. Big climbs, long miles, and all that fun stuff.
Ratings: ♥ **'Chilin' to** ♥♥♥♥♥ **'Killin'**

KOKOPELLI TRAILS
  Mary's Loop: ☺☺☺ / ♦♦ / ♥♥
  Horsethief Bench: ☺☺☺☺ / ♦♦, some ♦♦♦♦ / ♥♥♥
  Rustler's Loop: ☺☺☺ / ♦ / ♥
  Lion's Loop: ☺☺ / ♦♦, some ♦♦♦ / ♥♥♥
  Troy Built: ☺☺☺☺ / ♦♦♦ / ♥♥♥
  Moore Fun: ☺☺☺☺☺ / ♦♦♦♦♦ / ♥♥♥♥
  Steve's and Handcuffs: ☺☺☺ / ♦♦♦ / ♥♥
  Mack Ridge: ☺☺☺☺ / ♦♦♦ / ♥♥♥
  Grand Loop: ☺☺☺☺ / ♦♦♦ / ♥♥♥♥
  The Entire Kokopelli's Trial: ☺☺☺ / ♦♦♦ / ♥♥♥♥

BOOKCLIFF TRAILS
Prime Cut: ☺☺☺☺☺ / ♦ / ♥
Kessell Run: ☺☺☺☺ / ♦ / ♥
Chutes and Ladders: ☺☺☺☺☺ / ♦♦♦ / ♥♥♥
Zippety Do Da: ☺☺☺☺☺ / ♦♦♦♦♦ / ♥♥♥♥
Joe's Ridge: ☺☺☺☺ / ♦♦♦ / ♥♥
Frontside: ☺☺☺☺☺ / ♦♦♦ / ♥♥♥♥

THE EDGE LOOP
☺☺☺☺☺ singletrack (♦♦ road)
♦♦♦♦ / ♥♥♥♥♥ elevation & length.

FLIGHT OF ICARUS
☺☺☺☺☺ / ♦♦♦♦♦ / ♥♥♥♥♥

RABBIT VALLEY RIDES
The Western Rim: ☺☺☺☺☺ / ♦♦♦ / ♥♥
Kokopelli's: ☺☺☺ / ♦ / ♥
Overlook Trail: ☺☺☺ / ♦♦♦ / ♥♥
Overlook/Westwater: ☺☺☺☺ / ♦♦♦♦♦ / ♥♥♥♥♥
Zion Curtain: ☺☺☺☺ / ♦♦♦♦ / ♥♥♥♥
#3 and #4 Loop: ☺☺☺☺ / ♦♦♦♦ / ♥♥♥
The 'New' Rim Trail: ☺☺☺ / ♦♦♦♦♦ / ♥♥♥

GRAND JUNCTION RIDES
The Ribbon (long version): ☺☺☺☺☺ / ♦♦♦♦♦ / ♥♥♥♥
Ribbon/Andy's (short version): ☺☺☺☺ / ♦♦♦♦ / ♥♥♥
Eagle's Wing/Tail: ☺☺☺ / ♦♦♦♦♦ / ♥♥♥
Gunny Loop: ☺☺☺ / ♦♦♦♦ / ♥♥♥
Holy Cross Trail: ☺☺☺☺☺ / ♦♦♦♦♦ / ♥♥♥
Stagecoach: ☺☺☺☺ / ♦♦♦ some ♦♦♦♦♦ / ♥♥♥

HIGH COUNTRY RIDES
Turkey Flats: ☺☺☺☺☺ / ♦♦ / ♥♥♥
Wild Rose/Kannah Creek: ☺☺☺☺☺ / ♦♦♦♦ / ♥♥♥♥♥
Corral Fork to Little Creek: ☺☺☺☺☺ / ♦♦♦ / ♥♥♥

The making of a guide book

We built some cool trails in Fruita. Then we started to get more and more people coming to ride them. You know this, I know. So after drawing about 500 paper maps and telling people how to get to Mary's Loop it becomes apparent: we needed a guide book. Those are the origins of this book.

In 1996 for the first Fruita Fat Tire Festival I sat down and typed out a few sheets pf paper about the trails. We stapled them together at a print shop and the "Fruita Fat Tire Guide" was born. In 1997 I decided to get serious and actually measure some mileages and write a semi-real book. Days before the festival the entire files for this book were lost and the infamous 1997 edition had proof sheets as the pages complete with corrections and misspelling. I almost cried, but we somehow printed a book.

That stapled edition kept gaining rides and info and quality. But in 2003, with the help of Anne Keller, and Gary Smith from Pyramid Printing, we set out to do a "real book" and here you have it. Thanks for buying this book and for making this project actually succeed (I may cry again).

—Troy Rarick

ABOUT TROY

Troy returned to the area in 1994 after being away since high school. He founded the shop in Fruita and is tied by the ankle to most of the aspects of Fruita MTB life – Over the Edge, Fruita Fat Tire Fest, Edge Cycles and a wealth of fun singletrack sections. In addition to that, Troy is the father of two of the coolest kids in the world: Jordan and Danielle, and is married to Sarah, who will ride the legs off most of us.

But that's still not it. Who is Troy? Passionate and often "Over the Edge" in all he does. He is a fan of life itself and more than anything wants to win at that. They say we can't? Troy just might be the one to prove 'em wrong. If you happen to see a 100-mph cloud of dust coming out 18 Road it's probably Troy. Don't be mad, it's just the way he is. And as someone just said, "a little out there, but it seems to be working for ya:" always something new, a little bit challenging but in the end you loved it; that's Fruita Trails - That's Troy

ABOUT ANNE

Anne Keller, who was in charge of all hand-drawn maps, editing and layout of the book, has been a Fruita resident for two years, after a short migration across the 'Zion Curtain' from Moab, UT. Anne is currently making her mortgage payments and putting food on the table by playing the role of Sales and Soft Goods Manager of Over The Edge Sports. This position requires her to focus her energy on such fun things like creating t-shirt designs featuring half naked women (the Backdoor Café logo) and filling her head with all things 'bike geeky' in order to provide accurate and consistent information to all of our custom bike inquiries and sales. Anne's other life (which has been progressively making those mortgage payments easier, and the food put on the table a bit more upscale), consists of her artwork, both in the form of commissioned murals and canvases, and all things graphic and Adobe software generated.

ABOUT OUR SUPPORTERS

We would like shout out the highest 'thanks!' to all the other people who helped make this happen: Fred Matheney, Rich, Chuck Ibis, Ron Ige, Chips, all the people who told the tale of Fruita so well to so many, Sarah for all the work and help for all these years, Craven Daily and Pete Fagerlin for the awesome pictures they donated, Kevin, JD, Jon, Jen Z., and anyone else who helped with mileage and on-trail info. Thanks to Jen and Simon from OTE for letting Anne and me not work while we did this. Thanks to all in the local business community for your amazing support and teamwork. Thanks to the City of Fruita and Grand Junction (especially Barb) and the BLM, COPMOBA and IMBA for being the legs of the table and helping keep this dream alive. Huge thanks to all of you who have dirt under your nails from trail work. Finally, I personally thank you for buying this book and supporting our efforts here in Fruita. We couldn't do it if we had to get real jobs; thanks for the support.

Fruita Singletrack Rules!

Troy Rarick
Over the Edge Sports
Fruita Colorado USA
www.otesports.com

Anne & Troy in front of one of Anne's murals at the bike shop.